ANXIOUS ATTACHMENTS

ANXIOUS ATTACHMENTS

BETH ALVARADO

AUTUMN
HOUSE PRESS

"Autumn House Press" and "Autumn House" are registered trademarks owned by Autumn House Press, a nonprofit corporation whose mission is the publication and promotion of poetry and other fine literature.

pennsylvania
COUNCIL ON THE ARTS

Autumn House Press receives state arts funding support through a grant from the Pennsylvania Council on the Arts, a state agency funded by the Commonwealth of Pennsylvania, and the National Endowment for the Arts, a federal agency.

Cover design by Melissa Dias-Mandoly

ISBN: 978-1-938769-38-2
LCCN: 2018952006

All Autumn House books are printed on acid-free paper and meet the international standards of permanent books intended for purchase by libraries.

For Fernando

Let me call my anxiety, *desire*, then.
Let me call it, a *garden*.

Natalie Diaz, "From the Desire Field"

One must say *Yes* to life and embrace it wherever it is found—and it is found in terrible places. . . . For nothing is fixed, forever and forever and forever, it is not fixed; the earth is always shifting. . . .Generations do not cease to be born, and we are responsible to them because we are the only witnesses they have. The sea rises, the light fails, lovers cling to each other, and children cling to us. The moment we cease to hold each other, the moment we break faith with one another, the sea engulfs us and the light goes out.

James Baldwin, **Nothing Personal**

TABLE OF CONTENTS

IN A TOWN RINGED BY MISSILES   1

SHELTER   12

THE MOTHERHOOD POEMS   26

CLARITY   31

NOTES FROM PRAGUE   36

DAYS OF THE DEAD   45

STARS AND MOONS AND COMETS   57

ANXIOUS ATTACHMENTS   71

WATER IN THE DESERT   85

LOS PERDIDOS   95

ORDINARY DEVOTIONS   107

CAUTIONARY TALES   117

DIE DIE DIE   125

THIRTEEN WAYS OF LOOKING AT GRIEF   137

IN A TOWN RINGED BY MISSILES

Imagine turning your head and holding your arm out, as if for a blood test. You feel a slight prick, you loosen the tie, and then suddenly this warmth floods up; you feel a rush that begins at the base of your spine and surges up until it explodes in your head, like light. Then, for hours, you float in a bubble of warmth and well-being, dreams as vivid as movies drift before your eyes. This is why people like heroin.

Imagine you no longer feel like an ordinary girl, bland and vulnerable, but like a girl who is daring, an outsider, one of the guys.

This is why I tried it in the first place.

But *why* is a question that heroin addicts never ask. We know why. The question for an addict is *why not*? I had to have a very good reason to give up that rush. After all, I'd come to love the ritual, even the smell of sulfur, the flame beneath the spoon. I loved the liquid lightning that filled my veins and blossomed in my head. I loved the dreams, more brilliant with color than anything I'd seen in life. And then the psychic numbness that enveloped me for hours, where I had no worries, no fears, no anxieties, no guilt, no desires.

So *why* is not the question. We may as well ask why people have sex—which, as we all know, can have as-deadly side effects as heroin.

I was sixteen when I started. Thin, thin, always dressed in jeans and a black tee shirt, hair long and wild, I imagined I was a bohemian. The rules didn't apply to me. I didn't have to *attend* school to get As and Bs. Janis was still alive, I think, maybe even Morrison and Hendrix. The Civil Rights Bill was six years old. Watts had burned, so had Newark. John F. Kennedy, Malcolm X, Martin Luther King, and Bobby Kennedy had all been killed. Vietnam was old news. The Cold War was simply a part of the landscape. We wanted out. Sometimes it seemed as if the world were falling apart. We were kids living in the borderlands of Arizona, in a town ringed by missiles. We couldn't imagine a future. Instead, we shot dope. We ran it across the border. We were falling from idealism to despair. I'd fallen, needle to the vein. Planes like dark predators were circling overhead.

By the time I was nineteen—only three years later—I had not only grown up, I felt *old*. I had quit using every toxic substance I'd ever tried. This includes pot, hallucinogens, cocaine, speed, and alcohol, none of which required any effort at all to quit as I didn't especially like them, as well as the two that caused me difficulty, heroin and tobacco. I could claim that this makes me an expert, not only on addiction but on recovery—but I am ambivalent about everything: what constitutes addiction, whether physical addiction leads to psychological or vice versa, and whether or not people can be cured. I even wonder whether addiction is a symptom of an underlying disease or the disease itself.

Recreational use, that's how I thought about heroin when I first tried it. I wasn't going to get strung out. I just liked the high. Besides, I was a lightweight. I could get high on very small amounts, but eventually, after a few years, I did start using more often, several times a week, then every day, then several times a day. This is the point at which we considered ourselves strung out: we no longer got a rush, we didn't get high at all. We were shooting dope to keep from getting sick, to stay normal. And, frankly, it got boring. We were always having to figure out how to get money and then how to get dope. As boring as any other routine. I've heard both war and prison described as long stretches of boredom punctuated by moments of violence. That's a pretty good description of addiction. Nirvana, chemically induced, cannot last.

Out of all of those moments, and there were many, where people driven by desperation stole from us or pulled guns on us, there is one I remember so clearly that, in retrospect, I can call it a turning point. Franklin and Val had come over to cop, she'd just suffered her third miscarriage and, perhaps because of that, he let her get off first. Almost immediately, her eyes rolled up in her head and she hit the floor. She was out. Franklin was sitting on the bed, tying himself off. The whole time we were trying to revive her, Franklin was busy finding a vein. We slapped her, rubbed ice cubes on her, shook her. Nothing. We considered shooting her up with salt water, which we'd heard was the antidote, although we'd never seen it done. Finally, we dragged her to the bathtub and held her head under cold running water. When she came out of it, Franklin was still sitting on the bed, nodding. He rubbed his face. "Huh?" he said, looking at his wife.

That night, Fernando, who was not yet my husband, was lying next to me. We'd saved a tiny bit of dope for the next morning, but we had no money. Fernando said, "It's time to kick. Something bad is going to come down."

At the time, this seemed to me a profound statement and perhaps it was, implying as it did, cause and effect. Consequences. Lying there next to him, I knew what I couldn't articulate. The medicine had become the disease. We had fallen into a kind of despair, where we couldn't remember how we were before, where the things that happened seemed to happen to other people and we were numb observers, where there was no future, or if there was one, we couldn't imagine it.

But this is what I remember most about the day Val nearly died. It was a gray day, windy, dusty, bits of dried leaves in the air. After she came out of it, I watched them climb on their motorcycle. Franklin was big, tattoos on his arms, and Val seemed frail. She put her arms around him, leaned into him, and they sped off. I kept seeing her go out, lips blue. What if she nodded out on the highway? She would slip like a rag doll beneath the traffic behind them. He wouldn't notice. He wouldn't care. Could this happen to me? Where nothing nothing nothing would matter? Not Fernando. Not if I was pregnant. Nothing. Except dope?

Not long after that, Fernando and I decided to take a vacation from our addiction. This was something several of our friends had done. The idea was this: you went into a short detox program to bring your habit down, under control, and then you could start using again—recreationally—because you needed so much less. It was winter, 1973. There was an oil embargo, and we had to wait in long lines to fill the tank. It was difficult to drive around looking to score, and even more difficult to make a run to Mexico, and so, it only made sense to limit both our gas and our heroin consumption.

We went to a fourteen-day detox program at the Hope Center, courtesy of money set aside by the Nixon Administration. It was the first time I'd met addicts who were old, in their thirties and forties. They were parents. Some were pregnant. Some had school-aged children waiting in the car. Some juggled wiggling, pajama-clad toddlers as they stood in the morning medication line. I remember this old guy, Buster Glass, who Fernando knew from working construction. The first time Buster met me, he just started laughing. I was standing there, shivering and smoking in the morning medication line, my long hair hanging wet down my back, my bare feet in sandals, a thin sweater wrapped around me. Buster asked Fernando, "Who's this? Little Miss Granola Girl?" But I remember thinking, you mean this could be your life? This wasn't just something you did when you were young?

Tommy, our counselor, was small, quiet with dark skin. He used to say, "I've had my jones for twenty years." He'd been clean for the last two or so but he never gave himself credit for that. He counted all the years, from the first time to the present, as his habit. Any intervening years off dope didn't count either. "Once a junkie," he said, "always a junkie."

Questions Tommy asked us: Are you two a couple? Do you love each other or are you just spoon partners? Who leads and who follows? What's the worst thing you've ever done to get it? Have you ever betrayed each other? How did that feel? How far will you go? What lines will you cross? Of course, we couldn't answer all of these questions, but neither could we forget them.

One day, Tommy told me I was a self-medicating junkie. I didn't understand what he meant. He explained, "Something eats at you, you want to cover it up." But that seemed such a normal impulse, I couldn't believe it had anything to do with my habit. Our last day, Tommy held his hands in front of his face, his fingers pressed together. "Look at you two," he said to us. "What are you doing here? You have a chance to make it. You can fight this sucker. Don't give in."

He sighed, "It's going to be hard. You're used to hundreds of dollars passing through your hands every day, now maybe you'll spend $20, $10, that's all, groceries, gas for your car. You're used to excitement: you got to hustle for money." He shrugged at us. "Now you're going to be bored. Watch TV. What can we do, you'll say to each other. How often can a person go to the zoo? What do normal people do? What did we do before we got strung out?"

He looked from Fernando to me, back again, and then laughed, "You can't remember what you used to do, can you? Well, try. Because there's going to be only one thing you want to do and you can't let yourself do it, not even once."

He was right. Straight life was achingly boring, even worse than being strung out. Within three days, we were using again. But it was different. It was no longer unconscious. After that, whenever I got off, or convinced Fernando that we should get off, or was convinced by him, I had to admit I was rationalizing. This sounds very simple, but it seems to me that the ability to stand outside of myself and critique my own behavior and have insights into my own motivations was invaluable. I could no longer lie to myself.

I had been clean, completely clean for over three months when Fernando and I got married. I was almost twenty. We were living in his parents' house, along with his eight brothers and sisters. It was a small tract house on the south side of Tucson. Most everyone in the neighborhood, except for me, was Mexican or Mexican American. Even the Chinese people who owned the neighborhood grocery spoke better Spanish than I did.

In memory, that was a time of light, yellow light in the kitchen in the mornings as I sat with Fernando's mother and his younger brother and sisters at the breakfast table. A time of stories about La Llorona and the Mexican Revolution. This was when his mother began to initiate me into the family, when I began to believe that dreams did mean something, they could tell the future, for instance. Not only that, but two yolks meant twins. A fork dropped on the floor meant company was coming soon. You should make the sign of the cross when you salted the food. This was when I began to see that there was another world beneath this one, a world of spirits, a world where you made sense of the disparate pieces of reality by weaving them together into a story, a world where you paid attention to vague feelings that things "weren't right" and, by doing so, saved yourself untold grief.

Why I started using again, in that time of healing, when the self that had been dormant inside me—feelings, perception, my spirit—was waking up, I don't know. Maybe waking up was painful. Maybe it was the one last fall, the one I had to take before I could close my eyes on my old life, turn my back and say, no, that's not me. That's not who I am. At any rate, I had started chipping again, was into a little recreational use. I told myself I could handle it. I wasn't strung out but I was headed in that direction, even though I had an inkling I might be pregnant.

One day we went to a friend's house, a pool party, and while the others were swimming and drinking beer, we were in a back bedroom listening to *John Barleycorn Must Die*. I was sitting on the bed, I tied off, and suddenly, I was filled with the same despair I'd felt as I watched Val ride away on that motorcycle.

After I got off, I went outside and stretched out on a lounge chair by the pool; the light, a thousand flecks of white were bouncing off the turquoise water. Fernando sat down next to me. I closed my eyes. Someone opened the door and "Freedom Rider," that saxophone, flooded out. Fernando told me he wanted me to see a doctor. A doctor would tell me what I already knew: a not-yet-child was swimming inside, his eyes bulging, his heart beating, the veins in his delicate pink brain pulsing with the red veins on the insides of my eyelids. Fernando's hand was lying on my belly. Maybe, from inside, the eyes could see the shadows of his fingers.

And this is when I realized the truth. The lie I'd been telling myself was that if I didn't know, I couldn't be hurting it. I couldn't be responsible. But in that moment, I could see through the lie: the doctor pronouncing some words would not make it so and it would not make it *not* so. My knowing or not knowing changed nothing. If I was, I was. And, if I was, I might be hurting it.

Fortunately, I was not physically addicted. I did not have to go through withdrawals, which can be very dangerous for a fetus. In fact, with heroin, the withdrawals are more dangerous to the fetus than the drug itself and so a woman who becomes pregnant while physically addicted needs to keep using or to go into a treatment program so she can be gradually withdrawn. But I was lucky. Since I had already gone through detox before I got pregnant, I only had to fight the cravings, and that was hard enough. It was as if those months of pregnancy put me in a place where I was forced to remain drug free. Much like a rehab program might do, it gave me a hiatus from physical addiction where, I convinced myself, I couldn't do any drugs.

In a way, the craving was like grief. It could still overwhelm me at times, but at least it wasn't constant. I felt like I was moving out of darkness into light. My senses and feelings had begun to wake up. Being pregnant made me realize my body was important. Addicts tend to think of their bodies as "other" in a strange way. The body is not who they are. It is nothing, then, to stick a needle into it.

This mind/body split isn't unusual, of course. It's a fundamental dualism in Western philosophy. We think of it as normal; we learn to deny our bodies from childhood. I've heard the psychology of it explained this way: when you are a child, your feelings are who you are and when you are not listened to or are told to deny your feelings, you are learning to deny yourself. The message to you is: if my feelings are not important, then *I* am not important.

With addicts, though, the split must be magnified. I remember, when I was sixteen or so, staring at my arm, the blonde fuzz and the freckles, and puzzling over the fact that it was my arm, that somewhere inside this body, there was a me. Feeling the fetus move inside me, watching my breasts and belly swell, feeling the uncomfortable twinges of pregnancy, even morning sickness, made me aware of my physical presence, my skin, my veins, my breathing, my heartbeat. I had become essential.

It took me a long time to realize that the spirit isn't separate from the body: the spirit is *of* the body. The spirit needs the body to feel, to grow, to be with others, even to see and hear the world. The spirit is of the body, not separate from it, which is why death, any death, is a kind of violence.

Addiction disconnected me, not only from my own body, but also from those around me. Of course, when I was strung out, I couldn't see that my own behavior was what distanced me from others, even those who loved me. The truth is, I was so focused on my own needs that nobody else much mattered. Oh, I told myself they did and, to a certain extent, they did, but drug addiction is the ultimate form of solipsism. Even drinking is. There I was, wrapped in my own little chemical cocoon. Protected. Disconnected.

Even strung out, I had loved Fernando. Before we got married, he decided to go on methadone maintenance, which meant I either had to go on maintenance or quit chipping and stay clean if I wanted to keep seeing him. These were the Hope Center's rules, but I hated methadone and everything that went along with it, morning medication lines, dropping urines, attending group. So, I decided to stay clean—and I did, if you discount those few early slip-ups. I chose to stay clean. I chose Fernando, so we were already connected, but my being pregnant deepened our connection, committed us to one another, to the baby, to the family we were creating, in a way that marriage vows alone hadn't.

Living with his family mattered, connected me to his parents and brothers and sisters, made them my chosen family. Choosing to have Michael, to stay clean for him, committed Fernando and me to something larger than the two of us, than even the three of us, to something indefinable. We chose to put our connections to one another and to others above our own desires. This was not conscious, but it is what drew us back into life.

Pregnancy also allowed me to step out of the continuous present. I've heard that living in the moment is a good thing. There are books devoted to it but, for an addict, there is only the moment. There is no cause, no effect. No memory, no hope. No consequences, no foresight. You are suspended completely out of time. It's kind of like prison in that way: you go in, time stops, you come out blinking your eyes.

For example, when I got so pregnant I could no longer fit in my clothes, I gave them all away. It never occurred to me I might need them again. I bought no baby clothes, no crib, no bottles. About three weeks before I delivered, my mother and sister threw a shower for me. I remember holding one of those little gowns up. The baby became almost tangible. I embroidered two tiny tee shirts. My only preparation.

Yet pregnancy is the perfect metaphor for the future existing within the present. How could I be pregnant and *not* imagine a future? After all, once the baby gave me a swift kick in the bladder or swung from my ribs a few times, I had a sense of him as a separate being. My life went from being lived completely in the moment to being focused on the future. I couldn't imagine him, but I couldn't wait to have him.

This meant I had to project my "self" into the future, to begin to imagine myself as a different person, a mother, no less. This was not easy. To go from complete solipsism to *always* putting the baby first.

I used to tell Michael, when he was a teenager, that he had saved our lives. It might sound melodramatic, but I wanted to impress upon him and his sister that some choices can be irrevocable: you never know if you're one of those people who, like one of Fernando's brothers, might get hooked immediately. One time, and you're hooked. It seemed like the old myth was true for some people—or true enough.

Neither Fernando nor I ever got sent to prison. His brother, Marty, did. Everyone I know who's been there, male or female, is still an addict. I've never been there and, as I write this, I've been clean since 1974. This is also true of other people I know who didn't go, an unscientific survey, but revealing.

Prison does not cure addiction. In fact, there's such an ample supply of drugs in prison that a person could go in clean and come out with a habit. After all, what do we think happens when a bunch of drug users are confined in the same place and they have a captive market? They exercise a little capitalistic know-how, that's what they do. They're familiar with supply and demand.

The guards and visitors bring it in. In the '70s, in the state prison in Florence, Arizona, when Marty was first incarcerated at the age of nineteen, he said that the wars between the Mexican Mafia and the Aryan Brotherhood were over the drug trade as much as they were about race. This was a very violent period: there were murders and attempted murders weekly, if not daily. Legend has it that the head of the Mexican Mafia once stood out in the middle of the yard, brandished a pistol, and dared anyone, including the guards, to kill him: proof he was fearless and in control.

According to Marty—he has been in prison on drug charges three times and is still on methadone maintenance—many of the mostly white, middle-class addicts we knew frequent the same clinic he does, still addicted decades later. Only four of us, my husband and myself included, were able to quit in time to make stable lives for ourselves. Statistics are equally frightening: only one out of thirty-five addicts will stay clean and sober; some relapse after ten or fifteen years; many become alcoholics. In one study, of the 10 percent who had "recovered," half were counted as not relapsing *only* because they had died. Death as a cure—imagine that. I fit the profile of the heroin addict most likely to stay clean: young, female, addicted for under five years.

I always found it ironic that whenever I would admit I'd done heroin, people would ask me, But *why*? What *happened* to you? I was such a nice, middle-class white girl. They never asked Fernando the same question. Why? Because he was male, Mexican American, and had grown up in a poorer neighborhood? The assumption, especially back then, was that white people didn't do heroin. Even though plenty of white women and British poets had taken laudanum, the Victorian's favorite tincture—trade name heroin—most whites associated its use with blues and jazz players and so its stigma and the heavy penalties for its use were rooted in racist stereotypes. It's the same as with crack and cocaine: the tougher policing and significantly stiffer penalties for crack are also a reflection of systemic racism.

Ironically, Fernando hadn't used when he lived in the barrio. It was only later, after his parents moved the family into a white neighborhood that he hung out with anyone who was doing drugs heavier than marijuana. But the Vietnam War helped spawn a heroin epidemic—at least that's what they called it when use skyrocketed in the mostly white suburbs. All the guys we knew coming back from Nam were using China white. "This is some good shit," they told us. And it was. It was also deadly. In the four years I was shooting dope, sixteen people I knew died of drug overdoses or deliberate suicides. Sixteen people just like me. Middle-class, white. Children of doctors, lawyers, and restaurant owners.

I have read, recently, that the current opioid epidemic is the worst of the drug epidemics, with 64,000 dead from overdoses nationwide, in 2017. But listen to the language: opioid epidemic, before that, crack epidemic, before that heroin epidemic. The language is of illness and yet our approach is not treatment, especially not for the poor, especially not for those caught in the crack epidemic, who were more likely to be black and therefore were thrown into prison. Cocaine users, of course, were much more likely to get light sentences and to go to rehab.

When Marty got out of prison for the first time, in 1975, he told us to invest in prisons. He accurately predicted the soon-to-come prison-industrial complex and the ways that laws, especially drug laws, would be changed to incarcerate more people, primarily Hispanic and black males. At the time, we thought he was being paranoid.

Heroin *is* pernicious, of course. Some research indicates that people who get addicted to opiates may already have a deficiency of dopamine in their brains, which predisposes them to addiction to substances like heroin. But whether you're predisposed or not, if you use opiates with any regularity, you will get addicted because opioids take over a natural function of brain chemistry: they replace dopamine. When the drug stops, no dopamine, your nerves are screaming. Physical addiction is simple. If you don't do it, you experience pain; since you did it in the first place to alleviate or avoid pain, you just do it again. Basic Pavlovian theory. You know what cures you.

On the other hand, people who have abused drugs like methamphetamines or cocaine, which stimulate the pleasure centers of the brain, are always left with a need to have that center stimulated. Ecstasy, as I understand it, like Prozac, increases the amounts of serotonin in the brain and thus causes changes in brain chemistry, at least temporarily. In other words, even when there is no physiological predisposition to addiction and no physical dependency, because the drug itself causes changes in the brain, those changes can create a strong psychological addiction—in the case of cocaine or crack, to anything that will stimulate the pleasure center. So far as I know, cocaine is not physically addictive, only psychologically, but monkeys will give up food, water, and sex for cocaine. Monkeys will die for cocaine.

People die for cocaine. I once met a real estate developer who had lost everything—and he had quite a bit to lose—to that white powder. He said, "Cocaine is God's way of telling you that you make too much money."

But this is the interesting thing about the study of the monkeys with monkeys on their backs: the monkeys given unlimited access to cocaine died because they quit eating and drinking. But the monkeys who had unlimited access to heroin gradually leveled out their use. They still ate, they still slept, and they still had sex. They simply did enough heroin to keep from going through withdrawals. This experiment, which I read about in the *Stanford Alumna Magazine*, was published in the mid-eighties, when cocaine was still thought of as nose candy, something one might indulge in at cocktail parties, and the crack epidemic had just started. Whatever else the experiment's purpose, it did prove that there is no "just" to psychological addiction.

Physical addiction, therefore, no matter to what substance, seems to be the lesser of an addict's problems. Even if you have to take the old-fashioned route and go cold, your body gets over it. People do kick. Some stay clean for years before going back. It's the psychological pull, the craving, that's so hard to overcome. And the longer one uses, no matter what the substance, the fiercer the psychological addiction, yet I also assume that other factors—trauma, history of family dependency, unhealthy living situations, poverty, despair, etc.—make some of us more vulnerable in the first place.

For some people, of course, addiction *is* a symptom of an underlying disease; this is clinically known as a dual disorder. For example, many people with schizophrenia or bipolar disorders are addicts; prior to being diagnosed, they used (and became addicted to) illicit drugs in an attempt to balance out a brain chemistry that was naturally out of balance or had been thrown out by trauma. These are people, I think, who would not be able to stay clean without medical treatment and who, maybe, will simply need treatment for as long as they live. Fernando's brother seems to be one of these people.

Marty is a very religious person. He believed if he just had faith in God, God would help him stay clean. His failure, then, to quit only proved that he did not have enough faith; because he did not have enough faith, he was not worthy of God's help. This seems to me a catch-22 of the worst sort. The Higher Power I believe in gave me free will. Just as He didn't put the needle in my vein or the cigarette between my lips, neither will He take them out. He is not going to give me a magical fix where I don't *want* it anymore and, truth be told, that's the only cure any addict wants.

For someone like me—and, unfortunately, I'm not all that unusual—who began smoking dope and drinking at the age of fourteen, my whole sense of self, of who I was in the world was formed while I was under the influence of one substance or another. I saw myself as someone who was a risk-taker. I wasn't afraid of anything. But then I got pregnant. Suddenly I was someone who would poison her own child, someone who was not powerful but powerless, even over her own impulses. This juxtaposition caused me profound cognitive dissonance, a state that, according to Piaget and other theorists, is conducive to insight and therefore change: Who was I? I had to choose, to create a new sense of myself. And so, with help, I did.

Still, I sometimes wonder: Which was the defining moment? The moment I first felt chemical nirvana? Or the moment I chose to stay clean for Michael?

When I was in my twenties and thirties, I never would have admitted publicly to using drugs. I saw addiction as a moral failure, a failure of will. Out of fear and shame, I erased that girl, denied her, believed I had transformed myself completely. Now I can admit I am not so different from her. *Both* moments defined me. After all, a heroin addict is not so different from an alcoholic nor from those among us who need prescriptions to keep the darkness away.

There are people who can't survive, without help, the circumstances of their own lives. Is it any surprise that 85 percent of all women heroin addicts were sexually abused as children? And because all cycles are cyclical, there are men and women so broken they haven't been able to raise their own children. Lives so damaged, so hopeless, that self-destruction is a relief, that the idea of hitting bottom—or of "bringing the bottom up"—is a perverse joke.

There's always another bottom to hit. There is no voice so scathing as the one inside your head.

If I've learned anything from addiction, it's compassion, of the liberal variety, and so I want to ask what constellation of forces would have to come together to help people like Marty who, for years, self-medicated first with heroin and then with methadone? He's only recently been diagnosed as schizophrenic but he might have already had those problems when, at nineteen, the state threw him into prison for selling less than twenty dollars' worth of heroin to an undercover cop.

What happened there, we don't know, but he never recovered. He hears voices. He rarely leaves his small studio apartment. It took years for him to qualify for disability. Before that, he was homeless or we paid his rent. He's the big disheveled guy at the grocery store—you've seen him, you know him: the one you don't want to call brother.

SHELTER

Dina was the first child to come to the shelter facility. Fifteen, long brown hair hanging straight down her back, black eyeliner circling her eyes, she had been trying not to cry for hours, ever since her foster mother had announced no more: no more mud tracked across white carpeting, no more money stolen from the bowl in the kitchen, no more Valium missing from the cabinet. Dina and I were sitting on the low rock wall in front of the house, waiting for the foster mother to finish intake with the counselors. We were waiting for her to leave. I was holding my twenty-month-old son on my lap. Dina was staring at her feet. We were not talking. The foster mother had seemed upset. She doesn't want to leave you here, I thought to say, but how would that observation help Dina? And how did I know? So, I said nothing.

The house, a large California bungalow, had been built around the turn of the nineteenth century, two stories, a wide green roof, attic windows, and a deep front porch with stone pillars. When we first moved in, I sometimes imagined a girl in a white Victorian dress, her parasol up to protect her from the desert sun, walking up the steps for her piano lesson. Inside, her teacher would watch her through the wavering glass. Only thirty years later, I knew, during the Depression, Fernando's mother had walked up those steps. She was twelve years old, the nanny, there to help the woman with her small children, there to help fold the clothes and sweep the floors and wash the glass in the windows. Fernando and I found it ironic that we ended up living in the house where she had worked as a child. Her father, at some point, had built the wall of black volcanic rock that Dina and I were sitting on. That wall, its construction funded by the WPA, and walls like it, still wound up and down all the sidewalks in that part of Tucson.

Just west of the university, it was an older and once-genteel neighborhood, the stone walls squatting in front of the Victorians and California bungalows. By the 1960s, it had started slipping towards seedy: bars and head shops opening in some of the old houses; hippies and homeless children wandering the streets, panhandling from tourists and setting up camp in the park. By 1976, when the shelter opened, gentrification had begun: vintage clothing and used bookstores, vegetarian and ethnic restaurants, jewelry and pottery shops. You could get the future divined via the Tarot or the palm of your hand. Young families started moving in. Geraniums and wicker furniture sprouted on the large front porches.

The day we decided this house would become the shelter facility, we had just been hired and were standing on the front walk. Two men, three women, all of us in our early to late twenties. At twenty-two, I was the youngest, toddler balanced on my right hip. Fernando was standing next to me. He and I had signed on, in the late summer heat, 104 degrees easy, to be house-parents for $6,000 a year. The shelter was a revolving door, a temporary stop for runaways and other lost children. We were to shelter five at a time; they could each stay for a maximum of thirty days. The director, an ex-nun, and the two counselors would be on hand during the day, but the nights were all ours.

Maybe I thought working there would be a way of giving back. Maybe I had this idea that I could be noble, but what it meant, really, was that as house-parents, we got room and board, we could take classes, our son could stay at work with me, we'd be able to save money. We were qualified because we were ex-addicts, something that, even at the time, seemed laughable. We'd also been through training at Juvenile Court so someone had certified us, although in my heart I didn't feel certified to be anyone's parent, not even my son's.

On that particular August afternoon, from where we stood, we could smell something ripe, something dead. Inside, we found clogged toilets, closets fouled by transients, burned campfire circles in the carpets. Upstairs, a black dog, its belly bloated, legs stiff. Rigor mortis had set in. The house had to be cleaned, soiled green carpeting stripped from the wood floors, floors sanded and sealed, nearly a century of wallpaper scraped from the walls, walls painted white, ceilings pale blue with donated paint. The director declared that it would be the perfect bonding experience. We would emerge from this cleaning and renovation, a team. And we did.

Dina was our first. Before the foster mother, who was the guidance counselor at her school, Dina had lived with her mother and her nana downtown in a crumbling row house built in the 1800s. Her father, white, had never been a part of her life. Her mother was Mexican American. What was the rest of the story? Too much alcohol, maybe drugs. Maybe jail. Late at night, someone would tap on the window and the mother would disappear for weeks and then Dina would disappear from school or show up late, tired, stoned. The nana had been seriously ill, they found out. "Dina is asking for help," the school said. "That's what acting out is," the counselors said, "a cry for help."

Veronica was next. Tiny and dark-skinned, black eyes, her mother had been deported back to El Salvador. She lived with an old couple she called Nana and Tata in a small white house in the roughest part of town. A worker from juvie dropped her off. Domestic violence. Veronica had been accused of hitting the old lady, of threats. Veronica carried a sock full of change so she could make phone calls, one after another from the pay phone at the back of the house. "To her boyfriend," Dina whispered. "He's old. Has a car. He wants her to run away again."

My memories of this time are spotty. At least one hundred kids came through those doors, and I remember these first ones more clearly, these first ones before everything began to blur. Kenny, for instance, a handsome kid with dark curly hair and a big grin. Was he the one who started calling our Miguelito, Michael? Michael, Michael Motorcycle. Trish, blonde bangs falling in her eyes, she was the one who wouldn't bathe. She had been on the road for weeks, hitching rides with truckers. She smelled, kept her hair in her eyes, and no, she fucking was not interested in talking about it, thank you. Body odor had become her first line of defense. Paul, the redhead, had cut his father down when he found him hanging in the basement. Then his mother attempted to take her own life. Paul, on suicide watch, did not want to go to a boy's home in Phoenix. Kenny, too, was there for protection. His life had been threatened. One night during a drug deal gone bad, he saw them throw a blanket over this guy's head and then shoot him. "Why don't they call the police?" I asked, but Louis, the counselor, also an ex-addict, shook his head and clicked his partial plate in and out. "Kenny's father is going to take care of it," he said.

His father is going to take care of it? But it wasn't my job to ask questions. It was my job to see that everyone got up for breakfast, that breakfast was made, the dishes washed and put away, the floors swept, the vegetables chopped for dinner. We turned on the radio. Frampton, Aerosmith, Lynyrd Skynyrd. We threw open the windows wide. Made the beds. Ran the vacuum. Took showers and washed hair. Fernando and I took turns attending the morning staff meeting with the director and the counselors. The kids put their laundry in the washing machine outside, on the back of the house, then hung their clothes on the line. "Keep your eye out," I told them, "or the transients will take whatever they want. They are that quick!" Morning counseling sessions. Lunch, which was almost always make-your-own-sandwiches. Afternoon group. Family sessions. Then Fernando took the kids swimming at the Y or to play basketball. Michael and I went grocery shopping or we took a nap. Our days evaporated long before it was time to make dinner or tell stories. Our night-shift job was twenty-four hours long, it seemed, and weekends were included.

The nights. When the children came, especially if they were dropped off by the cops or juvie, they were sullen, or angry. Their hearts were crying: I don't get it. Why me? Why am I the—oh, just fill in the blank although it didn't appear on any intake form—the rejected one, the betrayed, the abandoned, the raped, the bruised, the fucked-up, the worthless, the loser, the stupid idiot, the ugly one, the one no one will listen to, the one no one wants or loves or cares about.

Actually, they never asked. Their hearts weren't crying. They were in a state of cosmic shock, chronic numbness. Their outrage was on hold. You mean things could have been different? Life wasn't like this for everyone? They sat on the couch. Middle of the night, middle of the day, didn't matter. They were quiet, still inside, watching, eyes tracking everything, muscles tensed. It was a matter of survival. It was dangerous to open up, to confide. Everyone first had to be measured. Everyone was found lacking.

When the kids came, they were assigned a bed. Boys downstairs. Girls, up. We always had more girls. They often called out an upstairs window and asked the street-people to bring them pot. I was young enough to look like them and sometimes, sitting, looking out of that window during afternoon group, I found out about the transactions when guys yelled up to tell me they had what I wanted. "I'm not who you think I am," I yelled down. "I work here, they're minors. You need to leave before I call the cops." "I'm going to pretend you're a potato," said one. "Plant you now. Dig you later." The girls shrugged. Like they didn't know what was going on, like they thought I'd never done anything like that. "No more," I told them. Those girls. From that window, which was right above our bedroom window, we could hear them trying to escape or the boys trying to climb in. When Fernando caught them, he made them climb back down. One girl, Connie, jumped out of the window because her boyfriend told her he would catch her. She broke his arm instead. Trish, I caught climbing out because she wanted to go to a wet tee-shirt contest down the street at Choo Choo's, a bar with a toy train circling on tracks near the ceiling and peanut shells on the floor. From our window, late into the night, we could hear people smashing beer bottles on the sidewalk, we heard the train just blocks away.

Michael, had we thought about Michael? He wasn't a baby any longer, but was not yet two. He trusted everyone. Reached his arms up to be held. Never one moment of anxiety about strangers. He was used to Fernando's big family, to being the center of attention in a world of teenagers. He jerked his head back in greeting, as if he were already fourteen and cool: "What's up?" Did we even think of him as a baby? Not even two. His dark green eyes and thick lashes, his feathery hair. His fat moon cheeks, dimples so deep people always asked him where he got them. Later, when he was older, maybe three or four, he would answer, inexplicably, San Diego. But then, when he was little, he shrugged. He knew only thirty-two words. He tucked his hands into the bib of his overalls and ran hooting and hollering through the big house. He was never afraid and, oddly, I didn't think to be afraid for him.

On the night Veronica ran away, we didn't want to call the cops. Instead, Fernando, Kenny, Paul, and Trish set out on foot, calling up and down the streets. They walked over to the park, where the street-people hung out, and up and down the dark side streets and alleys. "Ver-on-i-ca!" Dina and I could hear them. We were sitting on the back porch with Michael, our toes in the powdery dust, we were waiting in case Veronica came home. Then we decided to walk along Fourth Avenue, past the bars, their customers still raucous, music blaring, past the shuttered shops, down to the Dairy Queen where, Dina told me, sobbing, half an hour too late, Veronica was supposed to meet El Negro. Maybe it was a nickname, I thought. "She met him at the Spanish Well," Dina said, "that bar where the hookers hang out."

Dina carried Michael in her arms. We were both barefoot, wearing, proba-bly, shorts and tank tops, our long hair hanging down our backs. Dina's mascara smeared below her eyes. Maybe we both looked like junkies, like runaways. I felt something close to love, a tenderness, for her, but how can I tell you who she was? She has to be a character for you to remember her. What quirky things did she say? Did she tilt her head before speaking? Were her eyes a special shade of brown? Was her patience with Michael endearing? Did her weakness for getting high feel familiar? Her abandonment engender sympathy? But maybe she had been too marked by loss to be anything but timid, and so she disappeared and allowed me to project on to her, blank canvas that she was at fifteen, any characteristics I wanted. She was as willing as a puppy to do anything for love.

Sammy loved the cockatiel. It flew in the open window on the day he came to us and landed on his shoulder. He played pool with the bird perched next to his ear. He was fourteen and liked to show us a creased photo from his wallet: there he was, a skinny Puerto Rican kid standing with his arm around a plump white woman, maybe twice his age. "She sure be ugly," Paul said.

"What you think you be?" Sammy asked.

Trish put on eyeshadow for Kenny. I imagined her leaning forward over the sink, trying not to squint as the cigarette smoke floated up between her and her image in the mirror, smoothing the powder over her eyelid with her forefinger. Later, she'd lean back against the pool table. "How would I make this shot?" she'd ask Kenny, tilting her head so her bangs fell away from her eyes. "Is this how you hold the stick?"

"I can show her how to hold the stick," Sammy would say, elbowing Paul.

The pool table took up all the space in the room with the fireplace. You had to be careful when you made a side shot that the back of the cue didn't go through the side window, the window that looked out on the desert elm and the apartment next door. All night, shadowy figures went in and out of that apartment. They could have been selling drugs or offering sanctuary, we didn't know. During the day, we didn't see anyone, but we could always hear their radio, which sat on the bannister of their porch, tuned into a Spanish station.

Kenny would thump the floor with the cue stick whenever Trish was shooting. He would drape his arm over Dina's shoulders, whisper to her. "Check it out," he'd say, studying the look on Trish's face.

Was she jealous? Could he read her?

Sammy fiddled with the radio, Frampton, Boz Scaggs, salsa, static. He talked about how he liked to dance with the girls, like this, and then he'd grab Trish. She'd pull away. One night, he rubbed up against Dina's butt while she was leaning over to make a shot.

"In the kitchen," I told him. "Now. You can't go around touching the girls like that."

One eye wandered to the left as if his attention were divided. He ran up the stairs, climbed out the window and perched on the steepest part of the roof. He was smoking, looking out over Fourth Avenue, the trees and shops and street-people. He flicked his cigarette out in a red arc.

I worried every time he went out there on the steep, shingled roof, not only that he would fall, but because the house was a tinderbox. A wood house, seasoned in the desert sun for nearly a century, it would go up like that! One live butt left smoldering on that old roof was all it would take. There was a reason the fire marshalls had threatened to shut us down, a reason we had to boil water in big pots on the stove for baths and dishes until the hot water heater was replaced. A reason we would not be able to use the furnace in the coming winter and would have to chop wood for the fireplaces until the landlord—ironically, one of the children Fernando's mother used to nanny—made the necessary repairs.

For years, I would dream that I was upstairs with baby Michael and smoke was seeping up through the creaking floorboards. In the dream, I float out of the window, Michael hanging on to my long braid, floating behind me. I turn and gather him in my arms just as the house goes up in flames. Are the other children still inside? In my dream, it does not occur to me to wonder.

Sammy, his back up against the kitchen sink, paring knife in his hand, the circle of kids around him. Paul, his voice a sneer, "What're you afraid of, huh, Sammy? Let's see you use it."

Victim-precipitated homicide, the trainer from juvie had explained to us, when someone wants to die but doesn't want to kill himself, is a form of suicide often used by Catholics, for whom suicide is the only sin that cannot be forgiven. The Sin of Despair, it meant you had given up on God. Paul was Catholic, and this I knew, too, from the training: a child whose parent has committed suicide is 50 percent more likely to try it himself.

The girls backed up to the doorway. Michael on my hip, I grabbed Paul by the shoulder, pulled him back, away from Sammy's reach.

I imagined how Sammy saw us, the blur of our faces, our mouths opening and closing, our eyes narrowed and angry or full of fear. The sound of our voices must have been just sound, cacophony, louder and louder, urgent, but no words.

The arc of Paul's arm swung back towards me as he tried to shake himself free from my grip. I was afraid Sammy would lunge, the knife jerking up in his hand and cutting Paul.

And then Fernando's voice, deeper than ours. Calm. Fernando sliding easily, slowly, between Paul and Sammy. "Everything's gonna be all right, Sammy. You aren't in any trouble. Let's just go outside, that's it, no trouble."

Sammy pointed the knife at him but with no conviction. His face went slack. The kitchen silent.

"We were going to wash my car, Sammy," Fernando said, "Remember? You were going to help me wash my car."

He held his hand out for the knife but it flinched in Sammy's hand. "Okay, Sam," Fernando's hands held high in the air. "I won't touch you. You can keep the knife, but let's go outside. Come on, Sam. I've got those cigarettes I promised you."

The next day I heard Sammy yelling like crazy from the girls' room upstairs and I ran up to see what was wrong. "Lady," he said, "what's your name? Scream real loud," he said. "Please, lady. Sweet sugar lady. I wanna see your husband run up the stairs real fast. That girl, she did this to me with her finger"—and here he showed me how Dina had flipped him off—"and he don't say nothing to her."

Sammy had been kicked out of the last group home for molesting a younger child, Louis told us. He leaned back in his chair, and clucked his tongue. This was in the Monday morning staffing in the counselors' office, a large glassed-in porch. The fan swirled the smoke from their cigarettes; shafts of morning light sliced through the tamaracks along the back window. "That's DES for you," Louis laughed. "Just dropped him off. Tires smoking." He made a cuckoo sign with his finger and grinned. "Sammy's a quart low," he said.

Sammy had been flying pigeons on a roof in New York City; he'd catch one, tie a string to its leg and then fly it, around and around his head like a model airplane. That was when he first came to the attention of caseworkers. On his own at seven or eight. Sometimes he stoned the pigeons. Something about relatives here, something about Ritalin, but I kept thinking about the kid in the other group home, wondering if Sammy had used a weapon. Or had surprised the kid in his sleep. Face to the mattress. Thinking about Michael in the crib next to me all night. About the girls. About the bed checks I'd done, my bare feet on old wood.

DES, CPS, the police, all those government agencies. If they couldn't drop them here, where would they take them? Juvie. Lock-up. Detention. But sometimes, I thought, that was where they should take them.

A quart low. Two quarts low. Running on empty. Screws loose. That's how Louis talked, his jokes drawing everyone to him, making him the center of every room he entered. Chris, the other counselor, the one with the degree, told us that humor is a form of self-defense. "But watch out for transference. You don't want to get attached."

I won't get attached, this is what I told myself, and this was why. There were a few things that always seemed true about me. One, in moments of crisis, I never broke down. At times when others might be emotional, I swallowed. I chose not to feel but to observe. I tamped things down. The other was my ability to give myself over to fantasy, to love the fictions, the details of other people's lives, to have intense relationships for days or weeks or months and then to let go completely. For instance, when people died or went away, there were a few moments where a hole opened in my heart, a few days or weeks where I felt them hovering just over my right shoulder, but soon, I didn't even miss them. I couldn't imagine their faces except as they appeared in photographs. This is not to say I wouldn't later, sometimes, over the years, think of the kids from the shelter or check the obituaries. I would.

This staffing was the first I'd heard of molestation, and Sammy had been with us for three days—a long weekend. The screen door slapped shut as the kids took out the garbage, hung the throw rugs on the line. I got up and went into the kitchen, pulled Fernando into the pantry and whispered the news. "Goes with the territory," he said. "Good thing we do bed checks," he said. I looked over at Michael. Chair pulled up to the sink, he was helping Dina wash dishes. "Good thing he sleeps in our room," Fernando said. But I thought about this big house, all its rooms, how Michael sometimes disappeared from my sight. I took him back out to the meeting with me, where he ran back and forth between Louis and me, sitting on our laps or on the floor at my feet, drawing on paper with a pencil.

Angela had been meeting her stepfather in motel rooms. Again, in the morning staffing, in the room with two walls of glass, smoke swirling, I was told this story. But how much was memory and how much invention? Was her name Angela?

Did her mother bring her or did she come in on her own? She was a tall girl with long reddish hair and very freckled skin, ordinary in the way many girls are. There was a younger sister. Is this why she told? Is this why the mother brought her? Finally listened?

When did it start? She could have been six or even younger; she could have been ten, fourteen.

"Sometimes it's not rape, sometimes it's seduction." This is what Chris said in the meeting. "Sometimes the girl…" But what was the rest of the sentence? Is willing? Needs him? Wants him?

"But it's always a betrayal," I asked. "Isn't it?"

"Oh, yes," she said. "Yes."

And it may not stop then, I knew, even once she'd told. And that was another betrayal. And once there was that betrayal, especially by the mother, it was the same as saying, you don't matter. You are worthless. The child could do anything to her body, then, Chris explained. She could stick needles in it. She could prostitute it. Deprive it of food, burn it with a cigarette. Drown it in alcohol. Give her stepfather sexual access.

I didn't want to get attached, but I couldn't stop watching, which made me, what? A voyeur? Someone consumed with other people's sadness? But maybe it was because when I was their age, I wasn't conscious. I was anesthetized. I couldn't connect with myself, and so, maybe, in watching them I was hoping to learn something about myself. And there was a way in which I couldn't differentiate, especially with the girls. I knew how it felt to be them. Or I thought I knew.

Chris said they couldn't identify their feelings, they didn't know if they were sad or angry or confused. "They don't know how to name their emotions, we have to help them," she said. And I thought, but I don't know how to name them either.

Dina let Michael fill the tub with the hose. It was a round tin washtub, and she'd put it outside in the backyard on the one patch of grass. They washed Michael's doll's hair, poured the water from a yellow margarine bowl over the suds. I was sitting on the stoop in my sleeveless leotard and gauze skirt, my hair just washed, skirt pulled up between my thighs, the sun giving a sheen to the cocoa butter on my legs.

Dina braided my hair while it was still damp. "So it will have waves when it's dry," she said. Her fingers brushing my temples. I watched Michael through feathery eyelashes, my eyes squinted against the sun. There was a kind of halo on the water. It was hot, my skin reddening, white imprints of my fingers on Dina's arm, on Michael's shoulder, on my inner thigh. The desert sun, even in October, purified. Inside, in the cool, dark house, they were playing pool, the click of the balls, the hum of their voices, music drifting out of an upstairs window. Dina had to go to a group home soon. They'd found a placement for her. "Someday," I told her, "some-day, when I'm finished working here, I want to adopt you. I mean it. Absolutely."

Dina never told me anything about herself. I wondered if it was because she thought I couldn't possibly understand, because I was so different from her. But I knew how it felt to want to be numb, to want someone to listen, to want someone to love me. I knew how it felt to be a small speck of myself, to will myself into invis-ibility. Without words, I felt like I knew how it was to be her, but in retrospect, I'm not sure she felt that way at all.

Dina's nana lived downtown in the historic district. Barrio Viejo. In an old adobe row house on Main, the high narrow windows and doorways, corrugated tin roofs. We walked down streets shaded and quiet, past old houses, some abandoned, boarded up windows, sagging wooden porches, agave leaves unfurling out of the shadows like long tongues. The old corner grocery, no longer a grocery, had sheets across the windows. Past a house with white lacy curtains, geraniums flaming on a green windowsill. All of this in the shadow of the high rises downtown, their glass and steel and glint of the sun. "This house," Dina gestured to the cracked stucco of a house set back from the street, its plastered walls white behind a dark profusion of plants, "the junkies live here," she said, and then we were at her nana's.

Outside of the house, there were prickly pear cacti the size of trees. On the front porch, in coffee cans, succulents with pink flowers, portulaca. Her nana opened the door and the doorjamb was as thick as I could reach with my hand outstretched. Inside it was dark and cool, saguaro ribs in the high ceilings. Her nana stood for a minute, allowing her eyes to adjust. She was an old Mexican woman, stooped, frail, white hair escaping in wisps from a loose braid.

"Your mother, Dina," she said in Spanish, "she came by last week to see how you're doing."

She led us to the sofa where she took Dina's face into both of her hands. She was so old I wondered if she was Dina's grandmother or her great grandmother.

"They say I have to go to a group home, Nana." Dina lifted Michael to her lap. "But I want to come back here and live with you."

"Oh, *mi'ja*," her nana said, and then more sentences I didn't understand.

The cords snaked along the wall. Across the way, a high bed in the lone bedroom where all three of them had slept. Dina growing up here, someone tapping on the window at night, her mother rolling over in bed, holding the curtain back. Her mother, then, would leave in the daytime for work and stay out at night with her boyfriend. Or, I imagined, her mother would come home and sit on the floor in her robe, doing her nails, holding her cigarette, just so, and Dina would unwind the pink sponge rollers from her hair and let them fall in a soft pile on the floor.

"Her dumb boyfriend," Dina said as we climbed into the car, as if to ask why her mother chose the boyfriend over her. She played with the radio, punched it from station to station, turned it off. "But why can't I live with my nana? She's better now. You saw."

"It isn't up to me," I said.

"You know why," I said.

But I was thinking, what has Dina done that I didn't do at her age? Is she any more lost than I was? Why take her from her grandmother?

Dina turned her face to the blur of shops as we drove down Speedway. "Okay," she said, "so I messed up. I won't do it again."

I took Michael to visit Dina at the group home. She'd been there for two weeks and so she could have visitors. It was very clean and modern, not at all like our runaway shelter. It was corporate, funded by insurance, not grants. The furniture matched. All of the other girls were white. Even though Dina was half white and looked white, she wasn't, not really. Her accent was noticeable. She was the only ward of the state, the only charity case, in other words. The other girls were there because their parents had sent them, because they had insurance that would cover behavioral or mental or substance abuse problems. One girl was staying there while her parents toured Europe. The counselor, who was wearing a dress and nylons and heels, told me this, in Dina's presence, as soon as she greeted us at the door. Perhaps she wanted to make sure Dina was properly grateful.

She led us to a room with gold shag carpeting and gold brocade on the couch where Michael and I perched next to Dina as if we were suitors awaiting interrogation. "Can she go out for a soda?" I asked. But Dina wasn't allowed to leave yet, except to go to school. Besides, she was in trouble for smoking.

"Those are the rules. Same for everyone, Dina, you know that."

The counselor sat on a stool at the breakfast bar and pretended to read her newspaper.

Dina shrugged at my questions. She looked over at the counselor, rolled her eyes, and shrugged. Nothing more.

"Dina," I said, "try to make the best of it." I knew she wanted to come back to the shelter. She'd already been with us for two thirty-day stays. We broke the rules for her, but I knew they wouldn't do it again. "It's not for long," I told her. "Maybe you'll like the other girls if you talk to them. Maybe they'll find you another foster mother. Maybe. . ."

Her sidelong look. Still that thick makeup, a black line all around her eyes.

My mother was slicing sourdough bread, thin, and spreading it with butter and garlic. She'd come home to her house, where Michael and I were hanging out, to join us for lunch. It was our day off. (Last night, our night off. Eight vodka gimlets: two to relax, two to stop worrying about Dina, then four to stop seeing Trish in the cabs with truckers and Angela and her stepfather in the hotel room. I'd poked my cheek with my fingertip to make sure I was comfortably numb.) Michael and I had come over with baskets of laundry, but maybe, I told him, if the water is warm enough, we'll go for a swim. For sure, we'll walk up to the park. The neighborhood park, that was where I pushed Michael on the swings and caught him at the end of the slide and we felt like a regular mother and child on an outing—although, for him, a regular day, a normal day, must have now included several teenagers who sometimes needed as much attention as he did, if not more. (Angela said she couldn't remember when it started and then she told her mother and, then, the things her mother said.) My mother placed the bread under the broiler, added a few leaves of basil from her garden, large slices of tomato, thin slices of Havarti cheese, and then under the broiler again until the cheese was just curving down over the tomato, just bubbling from the heat, the bubbles edged brown. (Chris telling Angela's mother that the child might be the stepfather's or it might be from one of the boys in a shed after school.) I squeezed tangerines for juice, and then we sat at a card table in the square of light that fell through the sliding glass door of the family room. The lawn outside was still greenish; a resident family of quail scurried beneath the orange tree. Michael was lying on his stomach watching cartoons. He wanted a chocolate long john. How about cream of wheat, I asked him, or a cheese sandwich? He made a face. (Angela's mother crying. Angela afraid to touch her.) I closed my eyes and felt the sun on my back. Contrary to popular opinion, I told my mother, cheese sandwiches are great for breakfast. After we ate, she kissed Michael goodbye and then me, on the forehead, her lipstick waxy and perfumed. (I wondered if she could smell the alcohol oozing from my pores. I wondered if she thought I was a bad mother.) Her heels clicked across the linoleum. Michael climbed up on my lap and I wrapped one arm around him, felt his solid weight against my chest, rested my chin on his head. You smell like a puppy, I told him.

Veronica called. She'd had a baby boy. South Tucson, the air in winter was thin and clear, laced with the smell of burning mesquite. Veronica answered the door with the bundle, which was named LeRoi Jr. Teenaged girls, it seemed to me then, always named their boy babies after the father even when the father was nowhere to be found. At any rate, LeRoi Jr. he was, plump lips a smooth petal pink, hair curly, not that dark shock of hair that Mexican babies often had, his eyes a wide milky blue that would change to brown. Veronica gazed at him. She seemed calmer. The house was clean, the concrete floors, cold, tiled here and there, where the tile hadn't been worn away, with scraps of mismatched linoleum. All was swept bare. La Virgen de Guadalupe on the white wall. Her nana came out of the bedroom. She was not even as old as my mother, but she was heavy and walked with a cane. Veronica handed me the baby. The nana sat at the small wooden table, while Veronica scrambled beans and eggs for her. Heated a tortilla. The baby slept on my legs, his soft breathing, and curled fingers. Did I believe that having the baby had transformed her?

For me, pregnancy had been transformative. When Michael was born, my relationship to the world had shifted. In becoming a mother, I became an adult. But I was twenty. It wasn't easy. Veronica was sixteen. I had a husband, a mother, a mother-in-law, sisters and sisters-in-law. Veronica was on her own here. Her nana needed her almost as much as the baby did and being needed too much could become a kind of claustrophobia, I knew. This was why she had called, maybe. Maybe she needed help, was afraid of what could happen. Maybe she needed air, time to herself. The baby, his head fit in my hand; that was how small his head was; it fit in the palm of my hand. The layer of flesh, thin, the skin thinner, the soft spot pulsing. Everything about this baby was delicate, especially his skull above the concrete floor.

Christmas Eve, we drove over to the group home and Dina stumbled out to the car, climbed into the backseat next to Michael. She giggled and said she'd taken several Valium before she realized they were ten milligram tabs instead of five. Christmas Eve at Fernando's parents' house, his brothers and sisters sitting around the kitchen table, eating red meat tamales, nibbling pumpkin pie, then opening presents in the living room.

In the pictures, later, Michael's cheeks looked ruddy with fever, his eyes glittery. Why hadn't I noticed? Was I too preoccupied with Dina? Had I drunk that much wine? Dina. Rubber lady. Sliding down the arm of the couch. Should I have been worried about an overdose?

Christmas morning, the light was gray, the oranges on the trees in front of the group home looked fake. Dina sat hunched against the door of the car.

"I don't want to see you again when you're high," I told her.

"Fine. You won't."

Her face closed. I was turning away from her, already trying to forget. I knew, somehow, that I would never see her again. I knew she felt I was abandoning her, one person in a long line of many. And I was. There was no other way to think about it.

The car door creaked under its own weight, fell shut. The cold air closed behind her as she walked. The weak December light, the lumpy oranges on the trees in front of the whitewashed wall, the black wrought iron gate: in memory, all those are immediate and vivid while Dina's face has faded.

⁓ ⁓

This is what I told myself: the streets are *full* of lost children. Even their mothers abandoned them. Did you think you could be different? Save them? For how long do you think you will even remember their names? Dina, Veronica, Trish, Sammy, Kenny, Paul, Angela, Connie, Curtis (whose older brothers helped his father beat their mother until she miscarried), Rosemary, Gabby, Wendy, Brian, Alma (who loved another girl and so her parents kicked her out of the house), Manuela (the girl she loved), JoAnna, Doug, Moira, Todd (who, like Dina, kept coming back), Jeff (who will pull an empty gun on a cop, suicide by police), and then the girl, the Navajo girl, Barbara, who saw ghosts upstairs and so always slept downstairs on the couch.

There were others, many more, maybe a hundred others. But that spring, I will get pregnant and one of the kids, Jimmy, an eight-year-old pyromaniac, will threaten to kick me, "in the belly," he'll say, "and kill your baby." And I will grab him by his armpits and drag him across the picnic table. "Say that again," I'll tell him, giving him a hard shake, "and *I'll* kill *you*." And I meant it.

And I knew his history, I knew his mother was in jail again and that her boyfriend had started blowing pot smoke in his face when he was two. I knew Louis had just taken him off Ritalin, I knew the other kids had been teasing him, and still I meant it. With all my heart and gut, with both arms and both hands and my teeth, I meant it.

If I were another person, maybe I could have taken care of this child, these other children, and then gone home and grown basil or something. Cleaned the kitchen. I could have been noble and calm. I could have maintained some distance, maybe, or had a larger perspective. But I was not able to do that. I was often not calm or reasonable or understanding. My rage, as I was shaking that child, scared me.

We put in our notice soon after that and bought a small house from a Mormon family on the northwest side of town. Far from the shelter. I'd decided we should become exiles. I was tired, I guess, of being inhabited by others, which was what working with the kids at the shelter felt like. All of those children, their stories got lodged in me, and I could not dislodge them, not even from my dreams. I wished there were some way to transform their sorrows into song, so I could open my mouth and let them pass through me, become air.

But that was a selfish wish, and I knew it. It freed only me. I was thinking only of myself. Those kids, and kids like them, would still exist, they would still need shelter, and I, who knew this, was choosing my own children, as so many of us do, and then walking away.

THE MOTHERHOOD POEMS

On the birth of my first grandchild

The baby was born early. Eight weeks early to be exact. They now count gestation in weeks not months. I stood in the hall and heard his first cry, like a kitten mewing. He was small. Four pounds, three ounces.

For six weeks the baby is in neonatal ICU, which they say like this: Nick-U, as if it is a small university. There are monitors and feeding tubes and other tiny babies in their incubators. People look sad when they see the pictures of the baby, but he is our baby and we are not sad. Smaller babies are born every day.

Has the baby gone home? Has the baby gone home? Has the baby gone home?

The baby has a name, a long name. A first name, a middle name, a last name, but no nickname. To pick one would be presumptuous—on the part of me, the grandmother.

The baby has a thin neck but a strong one. He stretches it so he can look at the window. His eyes are sometimes open. His hands are big for such a small baby.

The baby has his father's dimples. We can see them now that he has gained weight. We can see them when he smiles. His father can hold two quarters in each dimple, for a total of a whole dollar on his face.

I guess we should say the baby has his own dimples. He has his own long fingers and feet, his own double chin and tiny penis. And, yes, we know: when the baby smiles, it's just gas.

Has the baby been strapped into the car seat of the back seat of the small car and hurtled down the LA freeways between SUVs and eighteen-wheelers? I want to call my son and ask: Has he been carried up the cement stairs? Did you cradle him in your arms? Did you hold on to the railing? You do know, don't you, that the rails of escalators in department stores are contaminated with germs, with yeast, with vaginal yeast, as in from the vaginas of strangers?

You will need to remember to wash your hands now. Please. You cannot wear flip-flops when carrying the tiny baby, not up and down cement stairs. Tell me you did not talk on the phone while driving.

On giving birth

The mother of the baby, my daughter-in-law, lay on the bed in the hospital for four days, trying *not* to have the baby. Magnesium dripped into her blood to stop the contractions. She had to lie on the bed in such a way that she didn't disturb the fetal monitor and its faithful record, the thump thump thump of the baby's heart.

On those limbo days, my son seemed so tall and his hair appeared especially black and shiny. He was utterly calm when he was with his wife, but when we left the hospital and he and I were alone, he zoomed into hyperactivity—talking to me and on the cell phone at the same time, walking fast, worrying. He said, "Love ya, bro" at the end of conversations with his friends. In California, everyone says "I love you" to everyone all the time. Is it a symptom of anxiety, an awareness of the tentative nature of life, or a habit?

Outside the hospital window, Wilshire Boulevard stretched sixteen blocks to the Pacific Ocean where the homeless men camped out on the grassy bluff above the beach and the Mexican peddlers sold them lone pieces of fruit and little bags of peanuts. Inside the room, my son and daughter-in-law were ohming and breathing. Sometimes her voice was strong, sometimes ragged with pain. To cry, to flee the scene, those were my strongest impulses, but I had promised my son I would stand in the hall. My job: to be the Center of the Earth.

Why was I so frightened for my daughter-in-law? Is Death always among the attending? Back home in Tucson, my sister-in-law, only forty, was in a drug-induced coma. Lymphoma. When she surfaced, she said, "Home." Hospitals are surreal capsules out of time and place. Britney Spears was down the hall having a caesarian. Men with thick necks stalked Labor and Delivery. Our baby was in distress. Paparazzi camped out front. The doctor, a tall British woman with long black hair, was firm. One more push would do it. "One. More. Push." The baby cried, such a small cry, but he was a tough cookie, our baby. He could breathe.

When my son went to the Nick-U with the baby, I was to stand next to his wife. They had to surgically remove the placenta, which had secured itself with scar tissue to the wall of her uterus. I threw myself over her and started weeping. I stroked her forehead furiously. "You can have painkillers now," I told her. "Demerol. Ask for Demerol. Please. This is no time to be brave."

On breastfeeding

When you are the grandmother, I tell myself, the baby is not your responsibility. Oh, you might get to sit on the couch and hold it occasionally, but it's not your fault if the baby is not getting enough to eat, and it certainly is not your fault if the lactation expert said to feed it with a syringe. "No more supplemental bottles," she'd said. "We want to avoid nipple confusion."

My son calls. "Don't worry," he says, his voice full of worry, "the baby's fontanel isn't depressed. No signs of dehydration yet." My daughter-in-law, I can hear the tears in her voice even though she isn't crying. "A syringe?" I ask politely. "Instead of the supplemental bottle?" (I excise from my voice any trace of alarm. I know I must be calm, reassuring, for I am the grandmother, the *paternal* grandmother, a whole different set of eggshells.) I go to Travelocity. I click Anytime. I scroll for flights. (Syringe feeding, I think. Who ever heard of syringe feeding?) "Tomorrow," I tell my daughter-in-law, "I'll be there tomorrow."

Oh, but I know how hard it is. The tiny baby has to open his mouth so wide. Almost like a snake, he must unhinge his jaw—for the breast, even the smallest breast, is larger than his head. He must take the whole nipple into his mouth and when the milk rushes down, warm and sweet, it must flood his mouth and his throat. He gulps. His eyes are round and, as yet, unfocused. Is it an adoring gaze or panic? Is he afraid he will drown?

His tiny nostrils are pressed against the flesh and I remember, with his father, pressing my finger, just there, near his nose, so he could breathe. All this: his fuzzy head, the pulsing soft spot, his round eyes and wild gulping, his grunting against my bare neck as I held him, waiting for the blessed burp, his limp body when he fell into sleep. Baby against my heart.

And all this I remember from my own son: the doubt, the loneliness, the fear no one can assuage, not even my mother for I am the mother now and even though I want to hide in the closet, 24/7, crying, I cannot. Someone needs me, a someone I don't even know. When I look into his eyes, he is a mystery. That's why his name doesn't fit him, and why no name would. Who is he? He gazes at me, but does not know me, except by the smell of my skin, the sound of my voice. He cannot see me and, because I am his mother, he'll never be able to see me, not clearly. Our beginnings are too close, skin against skin. This is a love affair, I'll admit it, I will never recover.

On the nature of babies

Does the baby want to be swaddled? Maybe he wants to lie face down on my forearm. Maybe he wants me to walk him up and down the hallway, my bare feet on the worn carpeting. Maybe he wants me to sway back and forth as I hold the pacifier in his mouth and watch television. Maybe he wants me to turn the television off. Maybe he wants me to sing little songs about his short life. This is what I did with his aunt, my daughter, who had colic and ear infections. (Oh, the drawing up of the knees, the jutting out of the bottom lip in pain, these are all so familiar.) Maybe he wants me to sing songs like those I sang to my babies: "House of the Rising Sun," "Down in the Valley," "Mercedes Benz." Drinking songs, down-on-your-luck songs, songs—it occurs to me now—that might be inappropriate for a baby.

Although, I must admit, this baby lives in a neighborhood where crime is common. His father, my son, was caught in the crossfire between the Armenian and Russian mafias. A bullet left a hole in his car. The clerks at 7/11 praised Allah for his deliverance. Which, while we're on the subject: When will the owner of my son's apartment complex ever realize he is a slumlord? When will he replace the carpeting? Fix the leaky gas stove? Repair the crumbling plaster under the window? Before the baby starts to crawl, please, and can ingest lead paint.

Oh, babies. They are like tiny birds. Voracious. They need milk, time, patience, jump seats, car seats, strollers, cribs, co-sleepers, changing tables, diapers, fire-escape ladders, onesies, sweat pants, sleep sacks, jumpsuits, coats, hats, and booties. They need bathtubs and baby wipes and baby wipe *warmers*. Plus receiving blankets, don't forget receiving blankets, you can never have enough receiving blankets. "Fold the corner down, just so," my son tells me, "to swaddle the baby." "You put him to sleep on his back?" I ask. "Not his tummy?" "The world has changed," my son tells me. (As if, at fifty-one, I am senile.)

There is a book I am supposed to follow but I haven't read it. The words swim on the page. The baby was swimming in the womb. When my daughter was little, I pushed her underwater to the swimming teacher and instead of going to him, she turned, her eyes open in water, and swam back to me. She was swimming without breath, back to me. She would drown to get back to me. There was the way the book said it was *supposed to be* and the way it *was*. This is what my daughter taught me: each baby sets the world spinning on a new axis.

My husband dreams he is holding the baby. The baby is so strong, he jerks back, pushes with his legs, and my husband drops him. Well, he almost drops him. It's a dream and so the moment of dropping is the moment of not-dropping. In dreams, life can correct itself automatically. So he doesn't drop him and when the baby is cradled in his arms again, the baby says, I still love you. Meaning, we guess, even though you almost dropped me. This is a dream about listening, we decide. The baby is trying to tell us something. But what? We don't know. "Maybe he wants more to eat," my husband says. "Maybe he wants us to visit."

If it were my dream, which it is not, the baby would be telling me: I am strong. It is okay for you to love me, Nana. Don't be afraid. No one will take me away from you. This is the fear and the baby knows it. He knows that his absence would be unbearable. He knows he has already taken root. He knows this. When I hold him and I stop singing, he cries. Soon, he will sing back to me. Oooo-oo, oooo-oo, he will sing, his voice against my neck breathy and demanding.

CLARITY

In the emergency room, my mother is flirting with the young, blond doctor. Dr. Dahling, I presume. Dr. Dahling, to be exact. "Right name," my mother says to me, when he leaves our white-curtained cubicle. We have been waiting for six hours in triage. She has been in extreme pain, but now, she flirts. She loves to flirt. She has always been a beautiful woman—Ingrid Bergman beautiful when she was young—and now, with her halo of white hair, still beautiful. It's her brown eyes, maybe, her bone structure, the classical symmetry of her features. But this doctor doesn't seem to notice. Until now, flirting has always served her well.

"Just as we thought," he will say upon reentry, after reviewing the X-Rays, "compression fracture of the spine. It should heal on its own in ten days. We'll give you painkillers. Do you want to go home or to a nursing home?"

My mother, of course, will choose home. Neither of us will realize he is sending her home to die, but he is. She has chronic lung disease, is on oxygen twenty-four hours a day. Even with pain killers, she will not be able to walk for twenty minutes a day, do her exercises, her breathing treatments; I will not be able to pound on her back to loosen the phlegm so she can cough it up; the phlegm, a soupy medium already full of bacteria, will cause pneumonia; the pneumonia will cause her lungs to fill with fluids, and she will slowly drown.

But at the time, we don't realize this. We are simply relieved to be released from the limbo of the emergency room. She is happy to be going home. I run for the car and the nurse wheels her out under the brightly lit canopy. I think: ten days. Okay, the semester is over. My class at the Poetry Center meets two evenings a week. I can handle ten days. I can come every morning, laptop in tow, and work in the spare room. True, I have papers to grade from pre-session. True, I have reports to write. True, I have to get ready for the conference in Prague. Yes, I'll have to make arrangements for someone to stay with her or for her to go into respite care. My sisters and brother have already said they cannot come while I'm in Prague, and so my mother and I have already talked about respite care, a "test drive" for assisted living, we called it. After all, we've checked out all the facilities, talked about the move for months: it is no longer safe for her to live alone even though I come over three or four times a week. We've agreed, so why does this feel like a crisis? I don't leave for two weeks. Her spine should be healed by then. Only three weeks, that's all I'll be gone. A test drive. We were going to do it anyway. Fernando and my friend have promised to visit her.

My mother is panting as I help her into the car. She is in pain. She hates my little foreign car, claims she can feel every bump in the asphalt, which she probably can. Also, she is afraid of accidents, prefers to be surrounded by heavy American steel. (I am her only liberal child and, for that, I know, she mistrusts me. She cannot understand why I would want to go to Prague, the dark sooty land of communists; she is afraid my daughter, who is going with me, will be kidnapped and sold as a sex slave.) She is hunched over in the passenger's seat, panting. From fatigue or pain? Both, probably. "Breathe through your nose," I tell her, "you can only get oxygen through the cannula." When she panics, she forgets and tries to gulp air in through her mouth, and here I am, paying no attention, running through the itinerary of my own life. "Deep breath," I tell her, "through your nose. Deep breath." I breathe with her: in through the nose, out through the mouth. I pat her bony shoulder and am surprised by its frailty. "That's it," I tell her, "we're almost home."

Can I rail against the indignities of old age? The thin skin, wrinkles, joint pain, chronic constipation, constant indigestion, urinary incontinence, memory lapses, loss of teeth, eyesight, clarity, and hearing, loss of mobility, stamina, and muscle strength not to mention the loss of independence. The normal decline of the body, I want to rail against it. My mother has little square metallic lenses in her eyes, implants from cataract surgery. They glint in a certain light. My mother, the cyborg. Eye appointments, dental appointments, heart appointments, lung appointments, bone density measurements, regular doctor's appointments. People treat her as if she were a child. "When was your last bowel movement, dear?" (They look at *me* as they ask her this!) "What is your birthday? What year is it? Who's the president?" They scold her for not having tests, not taking medications, not eating enough. For her negative attitude. Maybe she needs an attitude adjustment. Maybe she needs to exercise more. Maybe she needs to quit isolating herself. Maybe she needs to do crossword puzzles. Maybe she needs antidepressants, steroids, sleeping pills, stool softeners, beta-blockers, calcium supplements. Another inhaler? She refuses to take the beta-blocker. She would rather die, quickly, of a heart attack, than slowly of lung disease. (She may have memory lapses but you can't fault her logic.) She cancels appointments for crowns, telling the dental receptionist she doesn't plan on being alive long enough to get her money's worth.

Ten years ago, when she felt severe chest pains, she went outside and planted a rose bush from a graft, and then she drove herself to the hospital. All in one afternoon. To ensure that she would live, I guess. "No one who is planning on dying plants a rose," she told me later, "they require too much care." Sure enough, they found four serious clogs and admitted her immediately. Quadruple bypass. But she recovered. Took up watercolors. Went to the South of France to study the Impressionists. Then, when she returned, switched to Chinese brush painting, which became her forté.

Now, at eighty-five, she has chronic lung disease, an abdominal aortic aneurism—a time bomb according to our Dahling doctor—osteoporosis, hence the compression fracture. This is her third medical emergency in six months, the third time we've waited for hours in a hospital emergency room surrounded by people with germs, pain, trauma, and bored toddlers.

She is trembling as I help her from the car and take her into the house, deposit her in the nearest armchair. I switch her cannula from the oxygen canister to the compressor. I make her soup and toast, give her painkillers, put her to bed on the old white couch in her bedroom, a Duncan Fife; firm, the right height, she prefers it to the huge bed she shared with my father. The shadows from the bottlebrush tree fill the room. There must be a full moon.

I go to the all-night pharmacy because it's very late, to fill her prescriptions. There, in the green glare of the fluorescent lights, I call Fernando on my cell. I call my sisters. Each telling of the story gets easier. I feel my throat tighten, but my voice does not break. I sound calm. The pharmacist, a Middle-Eastern-looking man older than I am, peers at me over his reading glasses. "They're for my mother," I tell him.

"You cannot leave her alone," he says. "Not for a minute. She will fall. Then you will really be in trouble."

Sitting in the car, in the trash-strewn parking lot of the pharmacy, I call Fernando again. I watch the people who come out at night, harried parents with sick children, the homeless with their white plastic bags full of belongings, the night workers. I have a sinking feeling. This is serious. The pharmacist is right. She can't be left alone. Not for a moment. Why didn't I see this? When Fernando answers, I tell him I won't be home. Not any time soon.

Later that night, before she awakens, I am already sitting up in bed. It's as if there is a tether between us. I wake up, and I help her into the bathroom so that the cord from her oxygen won't get tangled in the wheels of her walker and trip her. Once she is back on her couch, I walk out to the kitchen to get her warm milk and another painkiller. Her townhouse is bathed in soft light from the atrium. The oxygen condenser hums, its red eye unblinking. This is all so familiar, I don't need to be fully awake. I stand in front of her while she drinks the milk and eats two saltines. The pill is her reward. She is so small, vulnerable as a child even if she weren't in pain. I lift her legs onto the couch, cover her, arrange her old pink cashmere sweater, just so, over her shoulder or over her feet, wherever she feels a chill. I kiss her on the forehead.

So, it has come to this, my mother, her human body, a shell. I lie on the edge of her bed, the shadows from the bottlebrush tree sway across the walls. Is this the end of clarity or the beginning? The end, when narrative breaks down, when reason quits its constant ordering of details, when emotion breaks through, breaks down, breaks? The voice breaks, that's what they say, and they mean with emotion. Or is it the beginning of clarity? When truth pierces denial and you see clearly: there is nothing you can do to make this end differently. It doesn't make sense, your mother dying, but that's what Fernando tells me. "The doctor sent your mother home to die. Without treatment, she will die."

My mother's legs, turning blue from lack of circulation. The rasping of her breath. The glittery feverishness in her eyes. The born-again caregiver who tells her that Jesus will straighten her spine. ("Hallelujah," I say, after she leaves. "She was a dim bulb," my mother laughs.) Vanilla bean ice cream, that's what we eat for dinner, the expensive kind, full of fat. "Why worry about cholesterol now?" my mother asks. Then there is the pulmonary nurse with short dark hair who agrees with Fernando's assessment. The florid GP who sends us to get an MRI and afterwards, in the dressing room, my mother coughing gobs of dark phlegm into brown paper towels I keep bringing from the bathroom; my mother coughing until I am flushed with heat and gagging, until she is so exhausted with pain she can barely sit, let alone stand. I leave her there, gasping, her tank almost out of oxygen, and run out to get the car, to move it to the front door. Back inside, I help her sit on the little seat of her walker, I fling the oxygen tank, her purse and mine over my shoulder, and then wheel her out into the waiting room full of people who will stare but make no move to help us. "Can't someone open the door?" I ask. Can't you help me get her to the car? Can't you see we are struggling? The walker is sliding sideways down the cement skirt towards the curb. "Please."

At night, after she is asleep, I go into the spare room. I lie on the bed and begin to cry. How did my life come to this? I want my big sister to come and fix everything. I long to go home and lie next to Fernando and hear his breath; I want to press my chest to his warm back so I can fall asleep. I am selfish, and I know it. My mother's legs are blue, her bad lung hurts, she is getting pneumonia. I email my sisters and my daughter. *The pulmonary nurse sent us to the GP, the GP sent us for an MRI, the MRI will determine if they can shoot cement into her spine to strengthen it so she can do her lung treatments, but the Invasive Radiologist will not return phone calls. No one returns phone calls. Soon she will be too sick to survive the procedure. Basically*, I write, *I am babysitting her while she dies.* Before I push send, I reread. Maybe I'm being a drama queen, an alarmist; maybe I'm just tired of taking care of her by myself; maybe I should just suck it up. But her legs are a purplish blue. I can hear the fluid in her lungs.

When my daughter comes to help me, she can see the pain in my mother's eyes. Kathryn sits at my mother's feet and holds her hand. She helps her walk from room to room. She stays with her while I teach. She calls the doctor's office every hour on the hour and leaves polite messages. She gives her little neck rubs, brings her chocolate chip cookies from the mall. She says the words my mother needs to hear. She says, "I cherish you, and I know you cherish me."

I cannot say these things. I cannot tell my mother how much I love her. Instead, I am cheerful. Because my mother does not want me to see her naked, I tell her I will wear dark glasses when I bathe her. "I'll wear dark glasses and shake my head like Stevie Wonder," I tell her, "then you can pretend I am blind."

As I stand behind her in the shower, she huddles on the small plastic seat. I am afraid she is cold. "Are you cold?" I ask her. But it is summer. I am dressed in my underwear and bra and my dark glasses and I bathe her. Still, she curves her arms, cradling her breasts. She does not want me to see my future. She is so small that my hand, outstretched as if to cover an octave on the piano, nearly spans her back, her skin, as thin and translucent as the water sliding over it. I can see her blue veins. Sometimes, when I sit next to her on the bed and rub her back, she touches my other hand. She asks me, "Is this my hand or yours?"

NOTES FROM PRAGUE

My friend Barbara is sitting on the small balcony in Old Town when our taxi pulls up. She waves as if she were welcoming us to a palace. Dlouhá Street. There is a youth hostel and a club across the way. The glass door to our entryway is cracked, the hallway dark and gray. The elevator is a wire cage with no door, an open fourth side, which makes me nervous. We crowd in with our luggage. Above us, the steel cable and pulley. Kathryn and I have come to a conference for photographers and writers where Barbara teaches poetry. In our hallway, I catch a quick chill from Cold War ghosts, but our apartment is full of light and blue furniture, polished wood floors. In the windows, floor to ceiling, white gauze curtains billow as if we are on the Mediterranean.

The streets seem full of people when we venture out. I feel the cobbles in the street press through my thin sandals. We follow Barbara, crossing the huge town square, passing below the Týn Church and the Astronomical Clock. We wind through narrow streets, past shops full of colorful wares and glaring lights. People stream by us. I feel disoriented. Already exhausted from the flight and from weeks of taking care of my mother before the trip, I have a sudden sense of my own fragility. I'm sure my feet will be bruised. There is no place smooth to walk. Girls are wearing flip-flops and high heels. This is what I'm thinking, of footwear, not of my mother whom I've left in a hospital, pneumonia and a compression fracture of the spine. No, I'm worrying about footwear, that my feet will bruise, that strangers' heels will get wedged in the spaces between the stones.

Kathryn takes my hand and pulls me close to her. She links her arm through mine. She can feel my distraction. And then we come around a dark corner to an opening. A street. Across it, a vista, the Charles Bridge, the black statues silhouetted against the light sky at dusk. Even though she hasn't brought her camera, I know Kathryn is studying the light. It is, Barbara declares, almost a perfect moment.

In the classroom, the teacher is saying that the subject matter must dictate the approach. You can't always get a single linear narrative. As in life, I think. The windows in the classroom are tall, wooden framed, and when the wind comes, they bang against the sills. When traffic noise comes, a student gets up to close them.

The first morning, I had been late to class and, in my haste, had tripped going up the marble staircase, bruising my shins. A few weeks later, taking the garbage down into the basement of the apartment building, I will slip on the cement stairs, bruising my tailbone. It could have been a very bad fall, but I'd grabbed the railing, wrenching my shoulder to stop the momentum. The first fall was due, I know, to my new glasses and my haste and the second to cement as slick as ice—either fall could have happened to anyone—but I still come to think of both as emblematic of my own aging, which I've never really felt before.

In the wide hallways, after class, I stand at windows, waiting for Barbara. Below, there is a courtyard and, one day, the photography students are lying on the ground. They are lying inside chalk drawings of human bodies. A crime scene? There is a man standing directly across from me in another window. He has a camera with a huge telephoto lens. He is taking a picture of the students. I have a sudden twinge of anxiety. I look for Kathryn. She is standing off to the side, watching. She wants no part of lying on the ground like a dead person.

Oddly, I am not worried that my mother will die while I'm in Prague. I believe she will wait for me. And this is true; she doesn't die. Instead she has an operation to stabilize her spine. She is treated for pneumonia and pumped full of morphine which, my sister says over the crackling phone, makes her demented. They have to move her to a private room because she insults the Jewish woman in the bed next to her. Or maybe it's the Indian woman she insults, or the Mexican—Fernando cringes all the same, but still, he visits her every day after work. Over and over my mother dreams that she is on Saipan, where she and her first husband were stationed in 1947. She dreams my older sister is a baby again and that they are surrounded by Japanese soldiers who, unaware that the war is over, have been hiding in the hills. Over and over she folds Kleenex, saying she is folding linen napkins for Kathryn's trousseau. Trousseau? It is not surprising that my mother loves such a word and loves the idea that Kathryn may someday marry someone who will expect her to have a trousseau with linen napkins.

One weekend, with other people from the conference, we take a field trip to Terezín. Even though touring a concentration camp seems to me obscene, I tell myself it is a way of witnessing history. What is the alternative? Forgetting, ignoring what is just beneath the surface of time? Terezín, an old fortress, is itself halfway underground. The bunk-rooms—what else to call them?—in bunkers. "Terezín was a holding camp or a transportation center, *not* a concentration camp," the guide tells us. "Those who died here," she is careful to say once we are all ushered into the bunk-room, "were not liquidated. They died of the con-ditions." Mostly children and the elderly were housed here and died here "of the conditions" or were sent from here to their deaths in concentration camps. Aus-chwitz. Bergen-Belsen.

The woman is saying numbers so incredible I know I will never remem-ber them. Four hundred slept in this room? The wooden platforms, where they slept, only so many centimeters allotted for each person. No mattresses, no blan-kets. The cold showers, the elderly prisoners made to walk naked, wet, across snow-covered yards, from showers to bunks. Emaciated. Starving. Weak. But not liquidated. Not yet. Pneumonia. Typhus, spread by lice. Tuberculosis, from the crowded conditions. All of this is told to us by a blonde woman in her early sixties, black-and-white print dress, in a soothing, lilting voice. She is solemn but it seems as if we are children, being told this information in the gentlest way pos-sible. There is no horror in the recitation of these facts, no outrage, no emotional register in her voice at all. How many times does a person have to say the word "liquidation" in reference to human beings before the voice loses its emotional timbre? Did she stand before a mirror and practice?

And, here, of course, I cannot help but picture my mother, her frail bones and thin blue veins, her sun-freckled skin, her modesty, my mother, her back hunched over, arms cradling her breasts, walking naked through the snow.

Kathryn is looking through her viewfinder through most of this, as if her camera can shield her from history. I am trying to absorb everything, to figure out how I am distancing myself. I feel nothing except for resistance to the woman who keeps herding us together for the recitation of the facts. There are: the bunks, the showers, the "fake bathroom" for the Red Cross and the media, rooms where people were tortured, round machines where clothing was washed but not at tem-peratures hot enough to kill lice. The beautiful grassy hill where the resistance workers were executed by firing squad four days before the war was over. The place where the escapee was publicly hanged. The place where three others successfully escaped. The long dark tunnel the resistance workers must have been led through to get to the hill where they were executed. The tunnel, the rough texture of its walls, the arched, barred windows in the corners where it changes directions.

Kathryn hangs back to take pictures, the voices of the woman and the group receding, wafting back. Kathryn and I, alone, and I am suddenly afraid, not of ghosts but of sensing them, of feeling what they felt. There is something unmis-takable in the air, something sacred. You can't believe they didn't know. You can't believe they walked through that long, dark, twisting tunnel, that they stepped out into sunlight and green grass, and didn't know.

In the museum we see the art by the children and their teachers. Some of the children survived, but none of the teachers did. And later, the crematorium that still smelled of ash. The room that looked like a medical room—the shiny stainless-steel operating table, the white enamel sink. This room particularly bothered me because I remembered reading about experiments performed on live prisoners without anesthesia—although that did not happen at Terezín as far as we know. As far as we know, according to the guide's lilting voice, only the dead were cremated here, not the living, only the bodies. Still, at the sight of the table, I suddenly feel my heart constrict, my first visceral response, other than the panicked claustrophobia in the tunnel.

There is an older man on the tour, traveling with his daughter—she is in her fifties, he in his late seventies, early eighties, maybe. He's having a difficult time emotionally. It seems to me that they're speaking Czech, but also, she speaks at times in English. When he emerges from the crematorium, he clutches at his heart. His eyes are tearing as they have been at several other points. I wonder if he is having a heart attack. I wonder if I am observing his emotional reactions to distance myself from my own. I know my father was cremated, I know my mother wants to be, but "cremated" is only a word until I smell the ash. I swear you can smell the ash.

I am standing outside, composing myself by looking at the trees, the clouds building above us. I am thinking of Hannah Arendt's *Eichmann in Jerusalem*, the banality of evil, of Susan Sontag's *Regarding the Pain of Others*, of Paul Celan's poem, "black milk of daybreak we drink you at night." Perhaps everything has to be mediated for me through language. Images, it seems to me, even photographs, are immediate, visceral, disturbing. Maybe the image, even when it's second-hand, an artifact, is imprinted in a primitive portion of the brain, a lobe that registers emotion or pain, that says, danger! run! Whereas language, like air, is literally taken into the body and so must be absorbed, must circulate with oxygen molecules in the blood, must become a part of the brain and, in that process, can somehow soften, dissipate, transform from raw emotion to meaning, abstraction. But then how to account for the difference between the phrases "banality of evil" and "black milk of daybreak"— even how and where they register in the body— since both are language?

As I'm sitting in the airless Bohemia Bagel Shop/Internet Café, I open emails from Fernando: *Your mother is recovering. Still thinks she's surrounded by Japanese soldiers. Lyn goes home tomorrow. Kay arrives Friday. Love to Kat. To you, too.*

When I recite his emails to Kathryn and Barbara, I insert the word "stop" wherever there's a period: "Your mother is recovering—stop—Thinks she's surrounded by Japanese soldiers—stop." We laugh. I feel almost giddy because none of this is my responsibility.

I cannot yet know that guilt is inevitable and will hit as soon as the airliner's tires touch the tarmac in Tucson. I cannot imagine the plans my mother will devise to escape skilled nursing and go back to her townhouse. "I'm going AMA on Monday," she will cheerily tell the nurses. "My son is coming to take me home." AMA. Against Medical Advice.

How can I imagine that my brother will need to believe her stories, need to believe that I abandoned her, almost killed her by putting her in the hospital? But this is his necessary fiction, the son as savior. She will convince him to rescue her by telling him the story about her brother Rees: when he found their mother in a nursing home, he walked in, picked her up right out of the bed, carried her out to his car and took her home. This, of course, as my mother knows it will, appeals to the romantic in my brother.

First plan: "He will come in an RV," she tells me, "and drive me all the way to Colorado."

"All the way across the Indian Reservation," I will ask her, knowing I am playing to her prejudices to discourage her, "with an oxygen tank? What happens if you break down?"

Second plan: "He will come in a Lincoln Continental," she says, "which has the smoothest ride ever, and take me to my townhouse."

"Who will take care of you there?" I ask her. "Phillip has to go back to Colorado. Lyn and Kay live in Colorado. Mom? I can't. I can't take care of you any longer."

How can I know I will be forced to be the wicked daughter, the one who has to tell her mother the truth, that she will never be well enough to go home, never be well enough to live independently? "Who will take care of you?" I am the one who will have to ask her this. She is sitting in her wheelchair next to the window. She is worrying a Kleenex to shreds. When I break down crying, she says, "I don't know why you have to be so emotional."

"If Phillip comes in here and takes you AMA," I tell her, "they can call the police."

"Will they arrest me, too? Think I'm guilty of collusion?"

"Mom, they're not going to put you in jail, but I know you don't want to see Phil get in trouble."

"Phil?" she says, placing her open palm against her heart emphatically. "Phil?" Again, with the hand. "*I'm* the one we're supposed to be worried about here."

She is the one we're supposed to be worried about. Oh, how I will chastise myself as I lie in bed at night. Ungrateful, selfish girl. *How sharper than a serpent's tooth. . .* But Phil doesn't know the rest of the story, how no one could provide proper care for my grandmother, how she ended up in a nursing home again, where she died, stroke by stroke.

This story, the real story, was never told to me when I was a child either. No, when I was a child I heard only the story of how my mother cared for her own mother, brushing her hair, day after day, the dutiful daughter giving up everything, even her singing, her art, for her mother. This is the story that will wake me up in the middle of the night in a panic. How can I abandon my mother? How can I choose my life over hers? But I will. And in calmer moments, I will know it is what she would have me do.

Barbara and I spend an afternoon just off Old Town Square in the Kinsky Palace, a pink building built in the eighteenth century although, once inside, you see remnants of the older building dating from the 1300s. We go upstairs to the National Gallery, its hallways and rooms filled with an exhibit, *Art Brut*. Not all of the artists were mental patients; some were recluses, their work found later in dusty, abandoned apartments. Many paintings were dream images, the eyes often haunting or frightening, bodies dismembered. Some reminded me of Basquiat, angular, full of motion, slashes of color. Words as images. Their materials: ink, pen, crayon, pencil, pharmaceuticals, blood, paper bags, pictures torn from magazines. One whole section of the exhibit was about the body, alienation from the body, fears about the body, fears about sex, fears about dismemberment or penetration, fears about the death of the body, and, of course, fears about the decay of the body. The artists' stories were printed on sheets of paper. Many had been abandoned as children or had suffered through the trauma of war. *Art Brut*. Raw Art. Visions of a chaotic world.

In the evenings, Old Town Square is filled with soccer fans waving flags. The TV is as large as the screen at an outdoor movie theatre. Barbara leads Kathryn and me through the winding cobblestone streets, over the bridge, up into the hills west of the Vltava River on a tram where we are deposited in a neighborhood that is much quieter than Old Town, more residential. Perhaps it is the Ukrainian District because there are so many shops with icons. Down the hill we walk. We stop at an outdoor restaurant in front of the monastery, the white tables set out in a row on the edge of a hill overlooking all of Prague. There is a breeze; the moon is peeking over the hills just to our right. We are even above the castle and the cathedral, the Týn Church in Old Town barely recognizable from this distance. We order ice cream and water.

Because this is a perfect moment, as Barbara would say, the kind of moment my mother would want me to have in Europe, I call her at the skilled nursing facility where she is recovering. Her voice is crackling or wispy; perhaps it is not a good connection. I walk over away from the tables, into the shadows, turning this way and that as if I am an antenna. I describe for her the moon, the castle, the river, the town square full of soccer fans. She says, "I called my sister Elizabeth. I told her you put me in a nursing home so you could take off for Europe."

My mother. I'd wondered how long it would take for that version of events to become her story. "But of course," my sister said, "But of course," Fernando laughed, "that would be the story. What did you expect?"

Beth put me in a nursing home—stop—she took off for Europe—stop—come save me—

Sometimes in the hot afternoons, I sit in the shade at da Nico's, a café with a green awning about two blocks from our apartment. The waitress wants to know, precisely, how much milk, how much sugar I want in my iced café au lait. Since she is so anxious about pleasing me, I worry that I seem like one of those picky Americans who wants everything to be exactly as it is at home. I am careful to praise the coffee and to leave a good tip. I always feel like an outsider in America, which is okay with me, but when I am in other countries, I feel very American. Case in point: the last time I was in Paris, 2004, Bush was visiting. The headline in *Le Monde*: "All of Europe Grits its Teeth." I carried *Le Monde* in my bag. I told Fernando we should speak to one another in Spanish while in cafés or on buses. I was tempted to take up smoking again, preferably Gauloise. There is a way in which I like being invisible. I like being surrounded by languages I don't understand. It allows me to exist in the world in a way in which I am not quite of it. Perhaps no one expects anything of me. And so maybe I could do it. Cut myself free. Never go home. Never take care of anyone else ever again. Rent a small apartment in Prague. Teach English as a foreign language. Become an ex-pat. Live the life of the mind. Maybe I am not too old; maybe it is not too late to choose another existence. Maybe no one would miss me.

A few nights earlier Kathryn and her friend Stephanie had gone to a five-story disco down by the river, but tonight we go out for a few drinks with the waiter from da Nico's. Phat Boy's, the bar where the locals hang out, is right around the corner from our apartment. The waiter is this little guy with short, dark hair, a fringe of bleached blond in the very front. He tells us that he lives an hour out from the restaurant. He makes 15,000 crowns a month or about $600. He says you make more only if you are a professional, an office worker, or work for the government, but he has a second job, which is finding girls who want to be dancers. He hooks them up with this man who sends them to other countries: Britain, Japan. "They make a lot of money," he says, "and in some countries there are very strict laws about not touching the dancers." London is mentioned, but later we are not sure if London has strict laws or not or if it has strict laws but they aren't enforced. In Japan, the men want to have sex with the dancers. He sees nothing wrong with providing this service. "The girls want to go," he says, "they make money, I make money." Kathryn and I look at one another. Could he be one of the sex-slave traders my mother was so worried about? It seems likely and unlikely in equal measure. He looks at Kathryn and Stephanie and laughs. "You girls like Nirvana? You girls like drugs and money and rock and roll?"

~ ~

In the classroom, I am sitting next to the teacher. I remember that we are sitting on a couch, which now seems impossible, but that's what I remember. We're sitting side by side, looking slightly to our left so we can see out the window that is just above the Jewish cemetery. Although I do not call him by his first name, it seems as if we are old friends, sitting there, musing about writing essays, about the difficulty of reflection, why it is nearly impossible under certain circumstances.

"The question is not what happens," he has said in class, "but what the writer makes of it. Reflection provides an essential counter-narrative, an ongoing dialectic between past and present."

He has also said that life has an underlying shape and that the writer's job is to discover the shape. Perhaps like a sculptor releasing the figure from the stone? I'm not sure I believe this. Life has a shape?

And then the thing I remember next also seems impossible, but I remember looking with him at Kathryn's proof sheets from Terezín. "So many doors," I say, "there were so many doors." Doors behind archways, doors behind bars and grids of bars, interior doors that led nowhere. "See?" I run my finger over the proof sheet.

I don't know if life has a shape or if I write to give it shape. I want to take things I've felt deeply and make of them moments the reader can enter. Memory as a place: Kathryn's and my room, the explosion of clothes from our suitcases, camera equipment hidden in clothes; Barbara's back bedroom with the leaky ceiling and small porch for drying clothes; gardens with hydrangea below; apartment balconies across the way, people smoking on them; the sidewalks of small white cobbles, some of which are used in our apartment as window stops; the white inlaid crosses in Old Town Square, twenty-seven, one for each martyr beheaded upon that spot. "The moment we step into the space of memory," Paul Auster writes, "we walk into the world." I look at the proof sheets, the long hallways full of doors half-opened, the windows behind bars, windows the shape of doors, windows and doors which are not openings, windows and doors which are sealed with heavy iron bars, doors the texture of tombstones, tombstones shaped like doors.

My mother hadn't wanted us to come to Prague. In the hospital, that's where she took both of my hands in hers. She made me promise to keep Kathryn safe. "Don't you let her out of your sight for a minute," she told me, both hands clutching mine. She paused. "But don't you bring her home early. Not even if I die." We held hands and I promised to keep Kathryn safe and she promised not to die and we felt as if saying it aloud would make it true. She had always said, show me you love me. Don't tell me. Words mean nothing. And I have tried to show her, by taking care of her. She had begun introducing me as her devoted daughter—"this is Beth, my daughter, she is *devoted* to me"—and, here, she would insert some detail about how bossy I am. And, even though she was joking, it was her way of saying, I know it's been hard for you. I've needed you. I appreciate what you've done.

In Prague, I am outside of time, my perceptions heightened by extreme emotion and sleeplessness. I stand in front of the long windows of our apartment; I part the white gauze curtains and look up and down the street for my daughter. It is three a.m. and I don't know where she is. Maybe the waiter has sold her to sex-slave traders. I have dreamed of that, of course, and of my mother, emaciated, helpless on the stainless-steel table. I cannot fall back to sleep. I stand before the long windows in my nightgown. Across the street, a youth hostel, a club. Behind windows like mine, young people come and go, up and down a staircase beneath a red neon arrow. Outside on the street, men stand next to their taxis. It is summer. Everyone is drunk and exuberant with noise. Teenaged boys run through the streets, waving flags, calling out *Deutschland, Deutschland.* I am in a country where I don't speak the languages, I can't sleep without dreaming of my mother's bones, and my daughter, where is she? I have promised to keep her safe. But where is she? I don't know. I stand in the window and watch for her, imagine myself walking the cobblestone streets, trying to find her. Imagine myself talking to people who do not understand me. Their mouths move in ways I cannot decipher. I place my open hand above my heart to calm it. I stand in the window and the taxi drivers below wave to me; they are so used to seeing me there, in my black nightgown, waiting.

Four months after we return, my mother will fall and break her hip and during the surgery, against her wishes, she will be intubated. In the hospital room, I will turn and see Kathryn's face close to my mother's. They are holding hands. Kathryn leans in to whisper so my mother can hear her, and the nurse says to me, "Oh, they look so much alike! Your daughter looks so much like your mother!" But it is their spirits we see. Kathryn and I have been sitting, each of us on either side of my mother's bed, each of us holding a hand. I have promised my mother that we will abide by her wishes; we will make them remove the breathing tube. "I have the strength," I tell her, "because of you." Her eyes, she closes her eyes then. Rests. She knows I will do what she wants. Release her. The spirit is of the body, I know this, it needs the body. But she wants to be released.

DAYS OF THE DEAD

A gray day in February, Fernando and I turn into Holy Hope Cemetery to look for his nana's grave. There is a woman standing there and I think she looks like family, like Patti, one of Fernando's younger sisters, but like Patti will look in twenty years. Patti in her sixties. It feels, for a moment, like a glimpse forward in time. Then the woman says, "Fernando?" And it turns out she is Toni, his cousin or his second cousin, the family lines tangled and forgotten in time. Fernando's mother is the only one who ever knew them, and now her thoughts are tangled. His mother has been visiting with the dead; they are more real to her now than the living. For her, long ago is vivid, and yesterday is easily forgotten. She comments on this often, says, "I can see them. They're so real, sitting there in my nana's garden, behind the high hedge, but I don't remember, *mi'jo*, have they passed on? Or are they still with us?"

Maybe this lapsed memory, this going back in time, is caused by a chemical or structural alteration in the brain. I wonder because my own brain is being altered by the toxicity of Interferon, an antiviral I have been taking for four months, and I am often sent off on trajectories not of my choosing. I think I must know what dementia feels like, even if I don't have it clinically: cobwebs in the brain, the synapses misfiring or at least firing differently, at odd angles. Maybe quantum physicists would say that this going backwards and forwards in time simply shows that time is not linear, but is a dimension instead. Maybe there are parallel universes and we walk through the dead or next to them with only the slightest apprehension, raised hair on the backs of our necks, say, a sudden chill, a quick blur in our peripheral vision. Maybe the dead are with us always but only when we are very sick or very old and ready to join them, maybe only then is the veil lifted, the doors of perception opened.

Or maybe it means, simply, we should have listened more carefully long before now. We should have listened before his mother's stories became fragments of memory, the grandmother from Italy—Petra? Pietra?—another grandmother, who came as a small child from California to Tucson by horseback when her family was driven from their *ranchos* and Spanish land grants by white settlers hungry for gold and land. Stories about Geronimo playing pool downtown in bars on Cushing Street while the soldiers were out scouring the desert for any sign of him, stories about Pancho Villa visiting neighbors in the middle of the night, stopping by for beers and burritos—but those must have been her mother's stories, not Dora's, because both Geronimo and Villa were dead by 1925, the year she was born. There was the story of the lamp with the red silk shade that Dora's employer had given her when she was twelve—she'd had to quit school, even though she wanted to be a teacher, so she could help support the family by being a nanny—how carefully she'd carried the lamp home, how carefully, even though her family had no electricity. This may have been when they lived in a tent, during the Depression, although the numbers seem all wrong—but what does accuracy matter? The story is really about the lamp's beauty, how much Dora's mother loved it even though it was useless, or maybe it's about the generosity of the woman's gesture, or maybe it's ironic, acknowledging the woman's let-them-eat-cake innocence or ignorance. Or maybe it's just a lamp with a red silk shade, the image of which has somehow implanted itself in my brain, that image triggering another indelible image: Dora as a girl, living in a tent near the base of A-Mountain, how they wet the earth and stomped it down with their bare feet until it became as hard, as smooth as any tile floor. Details from two different times confabulated into one memory in my mind, a memory of her memories.

With Toni is her boyfriend, Marcelino. They are cleaning the family graves, taking away the Christmas decorations and leaving in their place red and white silk flowers for Valentine's Day. Another cousin, Johnny, is buried here, next to Amelia, his mother, but his grave, although he died at least twenty-five years ago, has no headstone. It's still the plastic marker, cracked now, illegible. Toni kneels and takes the old flowers out of Amelia's brass vase.

I met Johnny when I was eighteen, first dating Fernando. It was 1972. Johnny's house was small and white, a shotgun house, one room straight back after another. I remember sitting under a tamarack tree watching his kids, all under six-years-old, run in and out of the front door. Johnny took care of them and fixed cars while his wife worked. He was helping Fernando repair my car, a '63 T-bird, or maybe Fernando's truck, an old Ford Flathead. Johnny could fix anything. If he couldn't find the parts, he'd make them.

His dad, a GI, had been killed in the war, and Johnny had been headed for college on the GI Bill, but there was a bad car accident, a serious head injury. And then he and Lupe married and had children right away. Some people, Fernando told me, thought Lupe was a witch or, at least, that she had bewitched Johnny. Maybe because she was so beautiful? Or because of all of the misfortune that had fallen on him? They wanted someone to blame? Fernando wasn't sure. He seemed to admire her. She worked at a dry cleaner, he'd said, one of the hardest jobs in the world.

By the time I met them, Johnny had been drinking too much for years, that and the worry of taking care of his children and the head injury—who knew why, exactly, but by then, he was already hearing voices. Airplanes could tune into his thoughts, he said, as they flew overhead. The cat in the alley was possessed by the devil.

It seems strange now but when I think about those days, sitting in a small house with mismatched salvaged windows, listening to him talk so matter-of-factly, mostly in English and partly in Spanish, it was as if I had entered a different universe where different rules applied. The mixture of languages had something to do with this feeling of suspended reality, I'm sure. I knew a cat couldn't be the devil, I didn't believe in the devil, really, or even that people could bewitch one another, but maybe I wanted to believe mysterious things were possible, that there was another more poetic way of being in the world.

Or maybe it was like reading. The stories replaced reality, *became* reality, at least as real in my memory as anything I had experienced firsthand. After all, the brain records a feeling of what happened and that emotion gives up memory cues—a word, an image, an impression—which we then have to translate into language in order to share. Memory, in other words, is always constructed: it is imaginative and transformative. Just as we have to imagine to read, we have to imagine to remember. For example, I'd always felt as if I knew my mother's mother very well, loved her, in fact, even though she'd died years before I was born and I'd never met her—or, rather, had met her only through my mother's stories, stories told with longing and with lots of immediate sensory detail. I guess I felt as if my mother's stories had happened to me in some way rather than were about things that had happened to her. Words as reality. Perception as reality. Suspension of disbelief.

If I believe your words, I believe your reality, and it will become a part of mine, the cells in my brain imprinted, physically changed by what I've heard. My other grandmother, for instance, my father's mother, when she was nearly one hundred, kept saying, "The greatest tragedy of my life was when my mother died when I was eighteen." But, in fact, this did not happen, not to my grandmother. Still, she told this story over and over. I thought it was true, until my father said, very loudly because she was hard of hearing, "Mother, your mother didn't die when you were eighteen." But this was her memory, it caused her great sorrow, and so maybe someone else's story had lodged itself in her mind and now, over and over, she suffered this loss. It was as if she had entered a room in someone else's life and it felt like home.

Words, images: we become unmoored in time, inhabit others' realities. Just think of Facebook: how years have disappeared as you've caught up with old friends, seen children you never knew existed; now you've gone on their vacations, know what they ate for dinner—it feels like you just saw them in the hallway at work, like time has stood still. Maybe some of those images will lodge in cells somewhere in your brain and when you're old, you'll believe you've been to Egypt with them, stood with your arms positioned just so, the pyramid behind you so that it looks as if you're holding it up, an optical illusion.

As we stand above Johnny's grave, I am trying to remember: when did he die? Lupe had already left him, but when, I don't know. She took the children. Then there was the time he threw all of the furniture out of his mother's house and washed it down with a hose. Someone called Fernando and when he and his brothers arrived, they drove his mother to a relative's house and left all the furniture in the yard to dry. They took Johnny out for a beer and they listened for a long time, just listened.

There are no dates visible on the little plastic marker. I don't want to ask, when did he die, because everyone else, even Toni's boyfriend, Marcelino, clearly remembers what I cannot. I know I must have had my own children by then, but in memory at the funeral I am still very young. I am still a foreigner, an outsider. There is a slight feeling of shock to this memory. I am trying to fully understand what is happening. Is it my first rosary? It isn't the first time someone I know has died, but maybe it's the first time I've seen a dead body. At the rosary, someone tells us they found him in the schoolyard. It was children who found him. When the cops got there, they said he'd probably walked into the crossbars of the monkey gym and knocked himself out. But everyone knew this wasn't true. The cops had been seen harassing him outside of a bar. They were the last ones to see him alive, someone said, and since when do you die from walking into the bars of a monkey gym? We could even see the bruises on his face under the makeup. Fernando and I went outside and stood with the old men while the women were inside whispering the rosary, inside with his children, now much older. Lupe was there, but I didn't talk to her. Probably Toni was there, but I don't remember seeing her.

So here we are. Holy Hope. Thirty years later? We can't remember the last time we saw each other. "Probably at a funeral," someone says. "Maybe at Albert's son's," I say, but then no one else speaks. Another cousin, Albert, his twelve-year-old was killed while playing with a stolen gun. I shouldn't have mentioned it. I have caused them all pain. There is a sense of shame when a child dies. Complicity. Neglect. We should have done something, we think, and, this time, it is not a vague feeling. That gun should not have been in that house. It is windy and overcast. Over to the south of us, a funeral. Military. The canvas ramada cover flaps in the wind. People are sitting beneath it in folding chairs as if at a concert. A man comes over to us and asks, in Spanish, if he can borrow a pen. He says they are burying a kid who just died in Iraq. IED. Four dead in the last month, just from that one high school.

Vietnam, that's Marcelino's era. Marcelino still wears his hair Pachuco style, slicked back. He has a round face and a crooked nose, maybe no teeth, his mouth sunken, but his eyes are the most amazing blue, the blue of a baby's eyes just before they turn brown, a smoky blue surrounded by a thin black line, as if someone has drawn a dark ring along the edge of his irises. When he and Johnny were kids in the late-fifties, only sixteen or seventeen years old, they hopped the trains to Idaho to work in the fields.

"It's a good thing we are telling these stories here," Toni says. "Johnny has been lonely."

We all agree. Everyone has been dreaming of him. Marcelino: that Johnny comes into his living room while he is sitting on the couch, watching TV, and Johnny says, come on, let's go up and buy some beer and Marcelino says he doesn't want to go and then Johnny leaves, walking alone. "Johnny could fix anything," Marcelino laughs, "he had ways of fixing cars with bobby pins and safety pins."

Fernando says, "Yeah, just when I can't get the bolt in, I think of Johnny, and in it goes. Like that."

But I know Fernando is thinking of his brother Marty. Marty has been dreaming about Johnny, too, and Fernando is afraid it means that Marty is about to join him. A heroin addict since he was eighteen, Marty's been on methadone for at least the past ten years and it's taken its toll: two types of hepatitis, bladder cancer. He smokes, oh, he smokes so much that his windows are brown, his teeth, his fingers. He's heard voices since the first time he got out of prison, almost thirty years ago, but we just thought he was religious. God talked to him, and since, as Fernando always says, there are no atheists in foxholes or prison, we thought he'd become devout. When people come from cultures that are religious or that believe in other levels of reality, the voices are not taken as a sign of illness, which explains, I guess, why we didn't think much of them. I mean, who doesn't hear voices? And what does it mean to "hear" voices? I can hear what my mother would say about most anything, her voice in my head as clear as a bell, no matter how far away she is in terms of distance or time.

Marty, like Johnny, heard voices, and they were alike in other ways: sensitive, handsome, always fell hard when they fell in love, inclined to addiction. Heroin, as it turns out, calms the voices—they've done lots of research about this in countries like England where heroin can be prescribed medicinally. Schizophrenics often self-medicate with heroin and after Marty had been on methadone for a while, it seemed like the voices escalated. It's impossible to know if that would have happened anyway, if it was part of the progression of the schizophrenia or if methadone simply isn't as effective as heroin, but because schizophrenics encode and remember information differently and because they have no sense of forgetting, they have no sense that a memory is not reliable. This, researchers think, is how delusions may get started: a memory, a voice, a piece of information gets called up. There is no sense of forgetting, no feeling that the detail is unreliable. It feels real; it is real.

Since it feels real, other details—some unreal, some real—also get called up, which is why the delusion might sometimes seem plausible in a strange way. Because Marty's stories were peppered with details of things we knew had happened, we often thought maybe the rest of the story had happened, too. It was possible until it became impossible: Marty started hearing the people in the apartment upstairs and two doors over plotting to kill him. The cop in his car over on the next street was looking for him. Filled with panic, he would call us in the middle of the night. One day he wanted Fernando to take him to the police station so he could confess past sins—sins Fernando was sure he had never committed. One day Fernando had to take the mirror off his wall to show him that no one was watching from the other side. This was not a two-way mirror. There was no hole, no camera. But reality, of course, was not convincing. Marty knew what he knew; he heard what he heard. It could be God. It could be a demon.

And if only he believed enough, God would cure him. To seek help meant he lacked faith, but, finally, the panic attacks were too frequent and too extreme, and so he listened when I explained dual disorder to him and then he decided to go to the mental health clinic. When Fernando picked him up, he was clutching a three-ring binder thick with evidence—he had been recording everything, what every voice said. Fernando asked him how it went, and Marty shook his head, "It appears that I might be crazy."

But now, who knows which is worse? We pinpoint the first break as coinciding with his first term in prison, where, since he was only nineteen, he was probably brutalized. Maybe he had a psychotic break, we don't know, but he was much changed when he came out. He must have suffered for years. We ostracized him—and for good reason, he stole from all of us—he was homeless, addicted, shamed, and all because he had no diagnosis. Diagnosis equals forgiveness: *oh, he was sick!*

Now he no longer has panic attacks; he's simply unconscious. The psych meds knock him out. Ironically, in many ways, they're worse for him than heroin. He sleeps all the time, has put on lots of weight, so much so that he has diabetes and can barely walk. Brain chemistry. All those years, it was just brain chemistry. Evidently, there's nothing mystical about it.

I haven't asked him if he still hears God or misses Him, although I suspect he might. I read once about an epileptic who stopped taking his medication because the seizures were ecstatic, as in the old religious meaning of the word. During them he saw light, he was filled with light, he came close to God. And so it was with some of the saints, I suppose. It seems like older ways of understanding visions and voices at least provided an identity and a place in the culture for people who, like Marty and Johnny, had them.

Toni, who has finished putting the new flowers on the graves, says she has been dreaming of Johnny, too, only in her dreams he is still young. Handsome. She thinks it means that whoever killed him has died or been arrested.

We are standing, now, in the old part of the cemetery, where the trees are huge and the stones are worn and pocked from weather. Fernando is helping Toni clean her parents' grave. She made sure her father was buried next to her mother, even though he had a girlfriend for years after her mother died.

"My mother's brother," I tell her, "was so angry at their father's infidelities that he dug him up. Then he opened their mother's grave—she had died years earlier and was buried in a different city—and put their father's casket under hers. To make sure he stayed put."

Toni laughs. "My dad met that woman at the mariachi festival. At Armory Park. She was one of those women, *tú sabes*, who never know what to do with their hair."

Toni is one of those women who always has her hair done, likewise her finger and toenails. She wears neat tailored clothes and carries a compact handbag. I am wearing cargo pants, a black tee shirt, and flip-flops. My hair, which is usually thick and wavy, has been falling out by the handfuls on this medication and so it is dry and wispy in the wind. I feel slightly accused, as if I am not only willfully unkempt, but would also steal the husbands of dead women. Of course, paranoia is also a possible side effect of the medication.

Marcelino motions with his head. His grandfather is buried over there, he tells me, in the potter's field, near the dry riverbed where, sometimes, during monsoons or heavy winter rains, caskets are washed out of their graves. I remember that one summer when the caskets were like boats floating along in the swollen waters of the flash flood and then, when the water subsided and the river was dry again, as it usually is here in the desert, they were left capsized, opened, the bones gone. Whose bones were where? But why does it matter? Bones washed clean in the water, bleached white in the sun, returned bare to the earth. It seems right somehow, that rain, which is sacred in the desert, would have such power. I think if they were my bones, I would prefer such a fate to a musty grave, and if God is going to resurrect me anyway, surely gathering my bones won't be a problem.

I hear Fernando tell Toni that my mother died four months ago, and I wonder if he mentions this to let her know that I have something in common with them, maybe no graves to visit or care for, but I have lost someone. And, yes, he's right. It is February; she died in November. I count. Four months. And it's been four months that I've been on this medication. One of the side effects is depression, evidently of the suicidal variety. If you feel like killing yourself or anyone else, you're supposed to call your doctor. But I'd refused to take the antidepressants, and now I don't know if I am feeling depression or grief or some combination of the two. I have never felt so weary, so hollowed out, so overcome at times with pure memory: my mother's hand in mine, her thin skin, my skin now thinning. "Do you want us to remove the breathing tube?" I had asked her and she had nodded, yes. "Even though it means we may have to let you go?" Yes. "Are you afraid?" No. When she died, her brown eyes became a purplish-blue. I saw it when I looked in them to be sure she was gone. I placed my hand over her eyelids, gently, but could not shut them. Since then, I have dreamed her only once. I dreamed I felt her hand in mine: She said, You haven't cried very much, and I said, Oh, Mom, you know how that is.

Marcelino says his grandfather's grave is always wet. I say, "My niece's is, too. She's buried next to a pond in Colorado and so her grave is always flooding—my sister says it's a good thing she was a swimmer." Marcelino says his grandfather hated to bathe. So maybe that's why. His grandmother used to tell them to chase him with a hose in order to get him to wash.

Marcelino tells me he was seven when his grandfather died. It was in the winter and then in the spring his mother had a baby at home. They cut the umbilical cord and tied it, but something went wrong with his mother and when they turned back to the baby, the umbilical cord had come untied and all the blood had come out. His baby sister was dead. So, his father went out and built a coffin, but it wasn't right, and so he built another and they put her body in it and then they drove out to the graveyard at night. Marcelino remembers the light from the lanterns. They dug up his grandfather's grave and put her in there with him.

"I still remember," he says, "we put her in there, but not so far down. She's there. My little sister. But there's no record of her. Not of her birth, not of her death. I'm the only one who knows now. Sometimes I want to go down and register her, but Toni tells me not to. It was illegal. I was a witness. She's afraid they'll arrest me."

Fernando and Toni have finished with her parents' grave and we move to her sister's and niece's—a few graves further over is brightly festooned with balloons and flowers and crepe paper. It's the little girl who died in the car accident on Christmas Eve, while she was out with her family delivering presents. Toni says they always keep her grave really nice. She talks about sometimes finding beer bottles or joints at her niece's grave. "*¡Aye, que desgraciados!* Don't they know this is sacred ground?"

As we leave, we all stop at a grave with a six-foot long headstone. Pictures of the husband and wife on their wedding day. A picture of him working on his motorcycle. The story of their lives engraved in marble, but the woman's dates are not complete.

Toni shakes her head. "It's bit much. Don't you think?"

"I don't know," Marcelino says, "I knew this guy. Pima Indian. They're buried with all their belongings."

Large screen TVs, I'm thinking.

Marcelino says he would take his riding lawn mower.

I imagine Holy Hope filled with detritus: half graveyard, half dump.

I would take my laptop, of course. My laptop has become an extension of my fingers because I have been typing with my eyes closed. My eyes, they get so tired on this medication. Macular degeneration is one of the side effects and so I'm afraid of blindness, fear it more than anything else, more than depression or even suicidal tendencies—because what would I do if I were blind? Probably commit suicide. My relationship to the world is visual. I love light, how it plays on the mountains and plants, changes the shapes and colors of the world. My eyes love the world. Maybe I should have been a painter, but my hands could never translate what I saw into images on paper, although they can—through the keyboard—translate my visions and memories into language and therefore into images. I sit for hours in a chair in my study with my eyes closed. I sit and I allow my mind to drift, to see memories, to form paragraphs, lovely little paragraphs, and then I sit at the laptop and, with my eyes still closed, record them. I am trying to record, to re-create, not only the memories themselves, but also what it feels like to remember, the process of memory.

I've read that when you're depressed, your memories become flat, generic. You adopt a "generic retrieval style." I'm not sure what that means. When you think "turkey," you get a generic picture of a turkey, like one in a 60s magazine, instead of a nuanced memory of one turkey with its golden skin and the moist dressing tucked inside? And your father smacking his lips and your mother sharpening the knife on that round thing before she hands it to him. And your little sister sticking her finger in the soft butter and your older sister mixing her peas in with her mashed potatoes. This is at the Newman's, I'm sure, the peas in the mashed potatoes, because someone makes a comment about how practical she is. We're seated on the piano bench at the end of a huge table in their basement and everyone is gathered around. They ask for someone to say grace, and I say the word, "Grace," and everyone laughs and I don't know why. I am six or seven and they are laughing but it doesn't seem unkind. This kind of memory is called "personal episodic memory" and it has a flash forward feature, which is called "episodic future thought."

In other words, to envision a specific future, you have to be able to remember a personal and specific past, and people who are depressed or schizophrenic have a hard time doing either, which means, I think, that I must be grieving and not depressed because my mind has been so fluid, inhabiting any time period at will.

In fact, I love the phrase "episodic future thought" and the idea it embodies: that to have a sense of the future, we must have a sense of the past, but also, that we make sense of the past through "episodic future thought," which I think of as foreknowledge or memories in advance or our sense of what things might mean depending on some sense of our future. And so, in a way, time is not linear or, at least, memory—which is how we experience time—is not linear. Memory is associative, a dimension where past-present-future co-exist and give one another meaning.

When I was young, I always thought that memory was like an object, something you might take out and examine and, in fact, people have thought, for a long time, that once a memory was consolidated and stored in long-term memory, it was static, unchangeable. But now they think that memories can be altered by the act of remembering, that they can reconsolidate themselves, which, if you're a writer, makes all kinds of sense. When you write about a memory, you have to leave out some details and emphasize others and so even in the act of trying to be true to memory, you have altered it—it's the written alteration that becomes static.

If you hadn't written it down, it would have gone on morphing, depending on new events, new knowledge, things others tell you they remember, and your understanding of the outcome. Every time you recall the memory, you might recall it differently—maybe even depending on the context in which you remember or tell it—and so memories are as plastic as the cells from which they're retrieved.

Memories, because they are constructed and reconstructed, will inevitably change. This concept explains to me something I had never understood: how my mother's stories of her past, even about her idealized childhood and her first love, could have become so dark at the end of her life. I'd always wondered how she could reconcile the differences for herself: how could her beloved, honored father of the memories she told during my childhood also be the philanderer who left her mother when she was dying stroke by stroke? It wasn't as if my mother had gradually and deliberately filled in darker nuances as we got older and could understand more, and it wasn't, I don't think, a sign that she had embraced the contradictions in his character. And it wasn't as if the stories were darker because she was depressed at the end of her life and could no longer view the past as malleable, although that would be the most obvious explanation. No, when she got older, it was as if she had erased the earlier memories completely, as if she were simply remembering aloud, no longer filtering, no longer shaping memories into stories for an audience. In some ways, I thought she was accessing memories she had never before allowed herself to access, as if she were confronting a "truth" she had once been compelled to forget, but was now compelled to remember and to tell before she died.

We are still standing in the old part of the cemetery, where the trees are huge, when we say goodbye to Toni and Marcelino. It feels as if we have been in the cemetery for hours, visited everyone we ever knew who passed.

Six months after we see Toni, Fernando's mother will die and we will bury her over in the newer part, a few rows down from her parents, from Amelia and Johnny, and the rest of a very large family. Her grave will be near a small willow tree and so it will always be easy for us to find. Dora will die at home with Fernando's father sitting next to her. They will wait for hours, until everyone has a chance to visit her and can stay with her for as long as they want before they call the coroner to take the body away. This is very comforting to me, for some reason, the thought that everyone wanted time to be with her body, even though "she" was no longer in it.

When my mother died, we left the room so quickly you would think we were afraid of the body. Only my daughter and I wanted to stay behind, lingered while the others hurried down the hall ahead of us; my daughter and I wanted to wait until they came to take her, we didn't want to leave her alone. It's still the only thing I feel guilty about, that I left her there, and all because my brother and sisters were in such a hurry to leave the scene of her passing and go home. This feeling of guilt is odd, because I knew she was no longer there, and so why did I feel so much tenderness for the body she had left behind?

When Fernando's mother dies, we will gather at her house, we will write the obituary together, we will gather photographs. At the rosary, we will see people we haven't seen for years and people I've never met and we will look at the pictures and tell stories and then, after the funeral, we will gather at Fernando's sister's house. We will all bring food, and we'll drink, and we'll remember together, for hours, with his mother's sisters and their husbands and their children, and so we'll hear stories we've never heard before and we'll make new memories about his mother and so it will be as if she still exists although we cannot see her.

It will feel as if she is watching us remember her—and maybe that comforts her, too, for surely she did not want to leave us—and it will feel even as if the others who have gone before have joined her in watching us, which means, we feel, that she is not alone.

When my mother died, she did not want a service and so, for me, something feels unfinished. Or perhaps her death simply feels unreal, impossible, even though I witnessed it, hastened it by telling them to remove the tube, even though I remember the details so clearly, so vividly. I have written about her, dedicated a book to her, a way of memorializing her, I suppose, but there has been no communal remembering and re-remembering and re-consolidating of memories, so no new memories have been made about her. In a way, it's as if, when she died, it was the end of memories, the end of her presence—which doesn't feel true of Fernando's mother.

Fernando seems to feel tied to the ground where his mother and his nana are buried. Even I feel a sense of calm when we visit. Sometimes a hawk flies out and greets us, and it feels as if some trace of his mother's consciousness is speaking to us. Fernando says we should go to my mother's favorite place, to Carmel, California, and have a picnic with our children and grandchildren and tell stories about her and about her sister, my favorite aunt, who lived there and whose ashes were scattered off the coast with her husband's. I think maybe we will, that maybe there is something to communal memory and ritual storytelling that is necessary.

I imagine the picnic table where we will sit, under tall trees, like these in the old part of the cemetery, but below us, there will be the ocean. I imagine the food, the crusty bread and salami and fizzy apple juice. I imagine my children's faces as they remember other picnics we had here when they were young with my mother and aunt and uncle. And maybe it will feel like they are watching, as if they're remembering, too. And even in imagining this, in replacing the image of my mother's body alone in that hospital room with the image of this picnic, I feel so much better. And I wonder, if I imagine this often enough, with enough detail, if I see Fernando standing with a baby in his arms, pointing out the seals in the cove below us, if I see my children cutting the baguettes and making simple sandwiches and pouring juice, if I see my grandchildren running around, picking up those big pine cones, getting their hands all sappy and dirty: when I'm very old, will I think it has happened? Will I have created a new room in my own memory, not from someone else's life, but from what I wanted in my own?

STARS AND MOONS AND COMETS

On a Sunday night in January 2013, around two in the morning, Fernando said, "Beth, you have to let me go."

And I said, "I love you, Fernando, but I let you go."

I said it clearly, in a loud voice, because I thought he might die that very moment, and I wanted our children to come into the room and be with him. Kathryn was asleep across the hall and Michael was sitting up talking to Fernando's brother in the living room. Both children heard and came into our bedroom and said, "Dad, we let you go."

Or maybe they didn't come in. Maybe it was the next night, when he actually died, that they told him, "We let you go." I can't be sure.

What does it mean to let someone go?

Sixteen months after Fernando died, I ran into my friend Susan in the hallway at work. She'd just lost her husband, and she compared it to being trapped in Dante's *Inferno*, which she and her husband had often taught together. She felt as if she were slogging alone through a dark wood and couldn't see ahead of her. "I just keep thinking," she said, "my husband is dead, my partner is dead, my beloved is dead."

I said I'd been "kind of out of it." Not terribly articulate, but it was true. I couldn't remember much from the recent past, and I couldn't imagine the future. I also couldn't imagine saying to myself, over and over, My husband is dead. Maybe Susan was trying to make it real for herself, but it seemed a kind of torture. Blessed was the anesthesia of disbelief—and of wine, and of his leftover Oxycodone, and of the Valium the doctor had given me so I could sleep.

"Why can't two people just decide one day that they want to die together?" I asked Fernando in 2000. Death was on my mind then because my father had just died and my aunt Dorothy was in hospice and my mother had a chronic lung disease and was trying to find a doctor who would promise to give her a massive dose of morphine if her lungs started to fail. She wanted to go quickly. She even quit taking her beta blockers, hoping her heart would give out first. In my family, we are more afraid of dying than of death.

"If you ever want me to kill you," I told Fernando back then, "I will." This was not a joke. I would give him morphine, heroin. It would be painless. "But," I told him, "you have to promise to do the same for me."

He wouldn't. He was a Catholic—a "recovering Catholic," as he put it, but a Catholic all the same. I came from a family of agnostics, although we considered ourselves Episcopalian.

After a day of taking care of my mother, I would lie awake at night and worry aloud that I was a bad daughter because I didn't want to take care of her. But neither did I want her to die. "Shhh," Fernando would tell me, even though he knew I hated to be shushed. "She knows you love her." His hand on my back let me fall asleep. This is one reason we get married: to have someone who can help us bear what we think we cannot.

When Fernando and I first got married, no one expected it to last, not even me. I remember thinking, as we walked in to see the justice of the peace, If it doesn't work out, we can always get divorced. In our wedding pictures, we both look miserable. It was 1974, and Fernando had cut his hair to chin length in honor of the occasion. I had hair down to the middle of my back and wore a long blue dress and a white sun hat he'd picked out for me. We'd bought our rings at a pawnshop, which seemed like a bad omen. Who pawns their wedding bands?

Later, looking at the pictures, I told Fernando, "I think if I'd said, *Stop*, you would have said, *Thank you*." And he laughed and agreed. Here's how he'd proposed to me: After a fight with my mother, I had shown up on his mother's doorstep, and his family had taken me in, even though there were already eleven people living in their small tract home on the south side of Tucson. His mother was Catholic, and then there were his sisters to consider. Fernando didn't want to be a bad influence. He told me, "If you're going to live here, we'll have to get married." That was it.

There was never any silence in that small house, with eight children, the TV, the radio, planes flying overhead, and the trucks on the freeway. We cooked and cleaned constantly. His mother mopped every day. Though the house was only a few years old, she had already worn the pattern off the linoleum. I got pregnant almost immediately after the wedding, and Fernando and I moved out, taking a few of his brothers with us. He worked construction, then started a house-painting business with his brothers to put me through school. He had no desire to go to college, although he'd always been a voracious reader. His buddies told him I would leave him as soon as I graduated, but I didn't leave. I got a fellowship for graduate school, and we both left, packed up a U-Haul and, with $500 in our pockets, moved to California, where he got a job running a painting crew full of undocumented workers from Australia, New Zealand, and Wales. When immigration officers showed up on the jobsite, they would go directly to Fernando and ask to see his papers. The irony is, he was the only one who was born in this country. Later at the bar, the other workers, with their thick accents, would joke that they were safe as long as they didn't open their mouths.

We had two children by then and became friends with other couples in married-student housing. Over dinner Fernando would have discussions about history and international politics with Moshe from Israel and Hans from Switzerland. "Isn't it funny?" he said. "Surrounded by foreigners, I feel fully American for the first time in my life." Away from his family, he'd realized that we were a family, just the four of us. By then we'd lost the pawnshop rings, and I'd had one made for myself: a gold band with stars and moons and comets.

On that Sunday night in January 2013, I had not been sound asleep when Fernando spoke. I had been lying awake next to him. I had loved him for forty years, ever since I was a girl of eighteen. I could hear my son and brother-in-law talking in the living room. Bernie, the brother my husband was closest to out of his four brothers, was staying the night in case we needed help. Fernando was over six feet tall and to get him to the bathroom was not easy. My daughter and I certainly could not do it by ourselves.

"Beth," Fernando said, "you have to let me go." He must have been gathering his strength to tell me this, because for most of the day he had been unable to speak. Was it the new prescription for Thorazine, or had the cancer gone to his brain? We didn't know.

Bernie's first wife, Martha, had died eight years earlier of lymphoma, and he was talking to my son about her. Kathryn, who was in nursing school, had promised her father that she would not let him die the way Martha had: in a hospital, hooked up to machines, swollen from chemotherapy, in a drug-induced sleep.

But his descent was so rapid—as if he had stepped off a cliff, is how Kathryn put it—that we weren't prepared. Earlier that week he had been walking two miles a day with me and complaining that I was starving him. Then on Saturday he suddenly didn't want to get out of bed, didn't want to eat. He slipped in and out of sleep as he watched football. We hadn't called hospice yet; he hadn't signed a DNR ("do not resuscitate"); we had no liquid morphine. Kathryn was worried he wouldn't be able to swallow pills, and therefore she wouldn't be able to ease his pain. We were afraid we'd have to take him to a hospital. We were afraid he would suffer.

Fernando was only sixty. He was going on without me, and I wasn't ready. Having witnessed my mother's death, I thought I was prepared for what would happen, but looking back I see that I was wrong.

That Friday, a few days before he died, a nutritionist told Fernando he could eat whatever he wanted. I had been trying to get him to follow a diet that was easy on the liver, since he had liver cancer, and on the gall bladder, since he had indigestion from the chemotherapy.

"Steak?" he asked her.

"In moderation," she replied.

On the way home I bought him a baguette piled high with lean roast beef, his favorite. We shared the chips and then took our walk. All the way up the hill he kept saying, "See, I told you I wanted meat. You've been starving me." I reminded him that we'd had pork loin two nights earlier, and that I'd just bought him a roast-beef sandwich. He said he wanted to stop and rest a minute—this was unusual—and I suggested we climb a little farther, to where there was a wall we could sit on and rest. "No," he said, "I just told you. I want to go back down the hill."

"Okay," I said. "Fine." I felt as if we had suddenly become a quarrelsome elderly couple, as if our old age had arrived that afternoon.

At night I would stand at the mirror and brush my hair and see a reflection of Fernando lying on the bed behind me. In the past he would have been watching me; he would have said something suggestive and patted the mattress beside him. But since he'd become so sick, he just lay there, sometimes with his eyes closed. He had been growing a beard. It was gray, but his hair was not. He was aging faster than I was, which made me feel young and vital, which made me feel sad and guilty.

If I cried, I did it in the backyard while he was napping. One day, I thought: I've tried so hard! The research, the coordinating of care, the double-checking of every doctor's recommendation, the reading about clinical trials, the careful planning of trips so we could spend more time with our children and grandchildren—I had been so brave through it all. But then I realized: This is not a test. No one is grading you. It's not even about you, really.

When I came back inside, he was up from his nap and had seen me in the yard. "You should cry more often," he said. He knew I wanted him to comfort me, but there was no comfort for this.

Only now, many months later, have I managed to think about the other times in our lives. The memories I can summon are snapshots, memories of memories, like the night we first brought Michael home from the hospital: When I woke up the next morning, Fernando was sitting in the rocking chair in his jeans, shirtless, the baby against his bare chest. I can see that. And I remember whenever Kathryn complained of a cold and didn't want to go to school, Fernando would take her to the convenience store and buy her little packages of Kleenex and cough drops, and then she would go. I remember how sometimes he would call me on the way to work and say, "Beth, you have to get up and see this sunrise." How his face relaxed when we went to the ocean for his sixtieth birthday. How he ate a pot brownie at Kathryn's house on our last Christmas and danced in the kitchen in his pajama bottoms and sweatshirt. "I am so happy," he said before we fell asleep that night. And he meant it, even though he was dying.

Had he lived, he would have taken his grandchildren to Rome and given them a tour of the Coliseum. Had he lived, we would have visited our friends in Israel. Had he lived, we would have gone fishing more often. I can project him into the future much more easily than I can summon memories of the days before his illness.

That last Friday night before he died, when Michael arrived from LA, Fernando told him that he wanted thick, juicy hamburgers and tacos the way his mother used to make them, the hamburger patted onto a corn tortilla and then dipped into hot oil. He wanted cheese on the burgers and pico de gallo and guacamole with the tacos. And french fries, and a grilled cheese for lunch. And fresh beans! With bacon! He wanted all the things the chemotherapy had prevented him from eating but that the nutritionist now said he could have.

On Saturday morning I heard the kids get up and leave for the grocery store to buy the foods he'd requested. Fernando got up, too, but instead of going down to the kitchen to make breakfast for himself and coffee for me, as he always did, he just used the bathroom and crawled back into bed, complaining that he was cold. I scooted over next to him, pressed my chest against his back, and rubbed his arm. I fell back to sleep, and when I woke, I asked if he wanted breakfast. He didn't think so. It was ten o'clock. Fernando never stayed in bed that long or skipped breakfast. I got up, but I didn't know what to do. I was standing in the hallway in my nightgown, crying, when the kids came in from the store with several pounds of hamburger we would never eat. Michael looked alarmed, but Kathryn had seen me like this before. "He's okay," I said. "He hasn't . . . It's nothing. He just doesn't want breakfast."

I am stoic, so when I say I was crying, I don't mean sobbing. I didn't want Fernando to see me cry, because he might have thought I had no hope. And if I had no hope, how could he have any? And if he didn't have hope, how could he possibly get well?

Driving home after the doctor told us Fernando had a year to live, he asked me if I was okay. I told him I was angry at the doctor for delivering the bad news in such an impersonal way, and he said, "Didn't you see? His hands were shaking. It was hard for him." I hadn't noticed. And I wondered: how had Fernando been able to notice?

"Do you believe him," I asked. "How can he be certain?"

"I don't know," Fernando said. "I just want to go to LA before the surgery. I want to see the boys play soccer." He looked at me. "It isn't time to tell the kids yet."

"Okay," I said.

He went back to work. I didn't know why. I thought he should stay home with me. Fuck work. Fuck his dull, boring job in a paint store, where no one was half as smart as he was. What a waste of his time, that job. What a waste of his life.

One day, months before the diagnosis, Fernando told me that a man who was probably schizophrenic had come into the paint store. The man was talking to himself in the second person: "Then you went there, and you did this, and they looked at you funny." Suddenly he turned to Fernando and said, "You're going to be dead within a year." This spooked Fernando, but I tried to dismiss it, saying the man was likely still talking to himself; he thought *he* was going to be dead in a year. But to Fernando it felt like a prophecy.

Another day an older customer came in and gave Fernando a ring with a cross on it that he'd had blessed at the Vatican. He said, "Here, you need this more than I do." Fernando kept it in his pocket.

Sometimes on our walks I would tell Fernando that I couldn't pray, and I didn't know what that meant. Did it mean I was willing to give him up too easily, or did it mean I didn't believe he was dying? When the doctors had first found the cancer, they'd thought it was stage I, and surgery would get it all. After the surgery they said it was stage IV. Every time we went to a doctor from then on, we got more bad news. Some nights, as we got into bed, I'd say, "I knew it. I knew it was a tumor. I knew it was malignant. I knew the surgery wouldn't work." And Fernando would sigh and say, "Let's not talk about this now," because night was when he prayed.

The surgeon said to Fernando, "Your liver is as bumpy as a toad."

The radiologist said she couldn't help because Fernando's portal vein, which carries 75 percent of the blood to the liver, was nearly occluded with a tumor. He had grown six new veins to compensate. She said, "The main freeway's been shut down for years, and you've been taking the side streets." If he didn't die from cancer, he would die from liver failure.

"It's heartbreaking, really," the oncologist told me. "He is so healthy otherwise."

"Live and let live," Fernando told me. "That's what I tell the tumors: 'I'll let you live inside me if you'll let me live.'"

He had almost died from hepatitis when he was twenty. At six-foot-one and 120 pounds, he was so weak his sister had to open the door to the doctor's office for him. He knew exactly how he'd gotten it: shooting up with an addict who was just back from Vietnam. He said, "Right after I got off, I looked at him and saw his eyes were yellow, and I knew. Oh, man, I knew." Fernando's eyes had turned yellow, his shit had turned white, and his piss had turned black. The doctor wanted to put him in the hospital, but Fernando knew his parents couldn't afford it, and so he went home to die. But his mother made him steaks. She rubbed her hands together and put them over his liver and prayed. His mother laid her hands on him and cured him. Now he was dying and his mother was dead and, although Fernando believed his mother had passed her ability to heal to Kathryn, he didn't want her to try. He said it would be too much of a burden. "But if God has given you a gift," I asked him, "how could it be a burden?" Finally, he let her try, and when she did, tears were streaming down her face. Later she told me, "All I could pray was that he wouldn't suffer." Then I understood the burden: It wasn't that she would feel pressured to heal him. It was that she would know there was no hope.

Fernando and I were at the beach, standing at the sea wall, looking out at the ocean. That's when he told me that every time someone he loved had been seriously ill, he had prayed for them to get well, telling God, "You can give them some of my time." He asked me now if I thought it would be wrong for him to ask God for that time back. "No," I said. "First of all, God is not an accountant. And second, why would God punish you for being generous? I never would have prayed for God to take time from me." And it was true. I wanted to live to be a hundred. He was hoping for at least one more year.

He had almost died from hepatitis when he was twenty. He had grown six new veins. In a way, he had been fighting for his life our whole marriage. We'd had forty years together—forty years we weren't supposed to have, with two children, and two grandchildren.

One afternoon on our walk I said, "Maybe we've already had our miracles."

It was that time of evening when the setting sun threw pink light on the mountains. He walked with his hands behind his back, as if deep in thought.

"I still want another miracle," I told him.

"Maybe," I would say, "you just have to envision a future." And he would look at the travel books I gave him and say, "Florence? Nice? Barcelona?" And we would sit together with the laptop and plan a trip.

But sometimes he would say (oh, so patiently), "Beth, you can't live without a liver."

Other times he would say, "I am dying because of the mistakes a twenty-year-old made."

I told Susan, the friend who'd lost her husband, that in the sixteen months since Fernando had died, I'd felt his presence more often than I had his absence. "Maybe I'm still in shock," I said. She said that denial is a coping mechanism. Susan was older than I was and had once been my teacher, so I thought she was probably right. Maybe my inability to believe he was gone was an attempt to cope.

But when I'd said I still felt his presence—was that true? It seemed as if I were talking about a belief in the afterlife, which wasn't what I'd meant. I had told him to wait for me, and I believed he would, but I didn't believe that I would see him again in a sunny heaven or sitting at Jesus's feet surrounded by sheep and small children, or that we would have our bodies again, or even that we would be recognizable, individual spirits with memories, identities, consciousness. I didn't know what I believed exactly. I just knew he would wait for me. It didn't seem possible for me to be eternally separated from him.

I still felt him like a warmth around my heart at times. I might be turning on the garden hose, and there he would be. One night I was crying in bed, crying so hard I worried I would have a heart attack. (This was actually why I wouldn't give in to crying: my heart always felt like a fist was clenching it, and I was afraid it would stop beating.) I couldn't control my sobbing, and I felt him get into bed behind me. I felt his arm thrown over me. I even felt his hard-on against my butt. And I wondered at the strength of his spirit: how strong must it have been to manifest itself so vividly?

I did not tell my friend Susan this. Nor did I tell her about the time I got into the car and said out loud, "Have I told you lately that I love you?" And then, when I put in an old Van Morrison tape, it stopped in the middle of a song, and there was a grinding noise as if the player were eating the tape, and then the song "Have I Told You Lately?" came on, right at the beginning, and I was sure Fernando was in the car with me, but I couldn't see or touch or hear him.

Once, in the middle of the night, I heard him say my name loud enough to wake me out of a drugged sleep. Sometimes I could feel him standing behind me, just as certainly as you can feel another person's body when he is close enough to kiss you on the neck.

I didn't quite understand the separation of the spirit from the body—the finality of it. When my four-year-old grandson asked me, "When is Tata going to be alive again?" I thought, Exactly. That is the question. Where is he?

~ ~

For a few years before his diagnosis, Fernando dreamed repeatedly that he was in a gray place with people who had passed on. Every time he dreamed about the gray place, it frightened him. He believed it was a portent of his death.

One night he dreamed he saw my mother in the gray place, and he said, "Margaret!" And she came up to him and put one hand on each of his shoulders and pushed him. She pushed him out of the gray place, and after that he didn't dream about it again. My mother knew I needed him.

"If I turn yellow," Fernando said, "that means I have a week, maybe ten days." I asked if he wanted me to call his brothers and sisters when that happened. "No," he said. "Why call them? I know they love me."

"But what if they want to see you?" I asked.

That Saturday before he died, I asked again if he wanted me to call them, and he said yes. I asked Kathryn and Michael to set about the task of phoning his father and his brothers and sisters.

Monday was Martin Luther King, Jr. Day, so it was a three-day weekend. For those three days, it was as if he were present at his own wake. People brought food and sat in the dining room and got out the photo albums and told stories. They visited with Fernando and then went outside and cried or talked about how awful it was or smoked a cigarette or drank a beer. They came inside and ate and took pictures of the old photos with their cellphones. The children ran around. We watched football. I talked to Fernando's sisters, feeling as if I were performing. His sisters thought he should go to a hospital and be fed through an IV, but Kathryn said no; she had promised to spare him that. He wanted to stay at home, to go quickly.

"There is nothing we can do," I said.

His sister asked, "Couldn't he have broth?"

I made broth. I put my hand on his cheek. "I am giving you broth," I said. I didn't want him to choke on it. I put some in an eye dropper and tried to feed him, squeezing it under his tongue. We wrote down the times when we gave him his pills. Someone brought swabs to moisten his mouth. He was still in the living room, so this must have been Saturday or Sunday. I put his medical records on the dining-room table, where everyone could read them. We still didn't have a DNR. Hospice wouldn't come until Monday. Kathryn had to help him move his legs when he wanted to lie down on the couch. She told him what she was doing before she would do it, but he couldn't understand her words.

"Dad," she'd say, "I know it's hard."

Once, as I was giving him water, he held up his hand and said, "Beth. Stop. Please." I think he meant, Stop pretending. Stop trying. Stop hoping. This is it. Finally, in these last moments, can we just admit it? I'm dying.

And I laughed. I don't know why. Maybe I was relieved that he was telling me to stop, or maybe I just loved that he could still respond, could still say a few words, could tell me what he wanted.

On Sunday we saw the hawk. I sat next to Fernando on the couch, and we saw it perched in the mesquite tree in the front yard. It seemed like a sign. Fernando had told me several times that whenever he went to visit his mother's grave, a hawk would fly down and greet him. I think he felt the hawk was a messenger from his mother, letting him know her spirit was near. When we used to go on walks, he would always spot hawks.

On my very last walk with Fernando, that Friday, we were not even a block from the house when I noticed a hawk in the crotch of a Palo Verde tree. It had a mouse in its talons. "Stop," I said to Fernando. And the hawk flew straight toward us, so close we could feel the air from its wings.

When we saw the hawk in the mesquite tree on Sunday, I said, "I don't think you're going to go to the gray place. I think you're going to go wherever your mother is."

That night we had to sit Fernando in a dining-room chair on top of a throw rug and then, pushing the chair and pulling the rug, slide him from the living room to the bedroom. We called it a "Mexican wheelchair." As Fernando and I got into bed, he said, "I am not going to die tonight."

In the hallway at work, Susan told me that she and her husband had gotten to talk about everything before the end, and for that she was grateful. I told her I felt gratitude, too: for a good death, for forty years, for my children and grand-children. In the sixteen months since Fernando's death, I had been cultivating gratitude. But standing there, I wondered if he and I had talked about every-thing. There was so much that had passed unspoken between us. Sometimes I'd thought I just knew what he wanted, but what if I'd been wrong? This worried me, now that I couldn't ask him. What if I hadn't understood him, or he hadn't understood me?

I said to Susan, "I feel like we are not yet untangled."

When Kathryn and I went to San Xavier del Bac Mission to light a candle in Fer-nando's memory, I started to pray for his spirit to be free, and I imagined a hawk soaring. But then, in my prayer, I thought, No. I am not ready for his spirit to be released. I still need him near me.

That's when I understood that I hadn't known what I was saying on the night before he died, when I'd told him, "I love you, Fernando, but I let you go." I still don't know what that meant. You can let the body go, because you have no choice, but the body isn't everything.

Maybe that's why we say, "I lost my husband." My dreams, right after Fernando died, were always of losing him: I was on a train trying to get to him, but I didn't know where he was, and my cellphone wouldn't work. I wasn't sad, only bewildered. I was sure I would eventually find him. Then one morning I dreamed we were making love, and he got up before I came, and I said, Come back here. I'm not finished. But he wanted to put the menudo on the stove and start the coffee. Come back here, I said again, suddenly angry. I heard him rattling the pots in the kitchen. I am so mad at you, I yelled, I could stab you in the heart!

One night he came to me in a dream. He was sitting across the room from me, at the foot of the bed. Beth, he said, I had been very sick for eight years.

When I woke up, I knew that was true. The last time he'd undergone a treatment for hepatitis C, in 2004, the doctors had taken him off the drug, because it wasn't working. He had seemed tired after that round of treatments. He had never fully recovered. And then I remembered: when my mother had died in 2006, I'd said, "No one else gets to die for at least six years." Why had I said that?

Recently I dreamed Fernando was very sick, and for some reason I was moving him from hotel to hotel, as if I didn't want him to be found. When I finally got him into a room and lay down on the bed next to him, he seemed frail. We were stretched out, facing each other. I could feel his breath on my face. Our lips touched, kissing quickly, as if there wasn't much time. And then I handcuffed my wrist to his so they couldn't take him.

After we went to San Xavier, I confessed to Kathryn that I couldn't pray for Fernando's spirit to be free. "I'm too selfish," I said. She said she hadn't prayed to God at all; she'd prayed to her dad. "Was that wrong?" she asked. I said that if she believed that God is in all of us, then, when she prayed to her dad, she was praying to God.

One night, shortly after Fernando died, Kathryn and I were sleeping together. Just as I was falling asleep, she asked if I had touched her forehead. She'd felt someone touch her there, the way her dad would have done if he'd tucked her in. I told her it wasn't me. It must have been him. And I rolled over and I felt sorry for myself that he hadn't visited me. I closed my eyes, and in a vision—not a dream—I saw my mother standing in a dark place, holding a lantern in one hand and opening a door with the other. Through the door I could see light, and I understood that he had gone there, to the light place. My mother was letting me know.

On Monday Fernando stayed in bed all day. He didn't go down to the living room. So if I remember something that happened in the living room, then I know it was either on Saturday or Sunday. If the memory takes place in the bedroom, then I know it was Monday. In the morning the hospice nurse came, and I signed the DNR, and she explained the use of the morphine and the sedative and what to look for to tell whether death was near. Then Kathryn, Michael, and I all went back to the bedroom with the nurse, and she asked if we had any scissors. I got a pair, and we cut Fernando out of his pajamas and put a hospital gown on him. "I'm cold," he said. "I can't feel my legs." I asked him if he was afraid, and he said no.

Outside the bedroom, the hospice nurse told Michael it could still be days—weeks, even. I started to panic then. "What if Kathryn and I can't take care of him by ourselves? Isn't there a bed for him in the hospice?" The answer was No. The hospice was evidently a service, not a place to which he could be taken. And if we took him to the hospital, doctors would prolong the dying process. Michael and my brother-in-law Bernie had been helping us move Fernando, but they couldn't stay. "We can't move him by ourselves," I told the nurse. And she explained that sometimes an eighty-five-year-old woman has to take care of her dying husband by herself. "How does she do that?" I asked. The hospice nurse said she didn't know.

At one point that afternoon, I decided to lie down next to Fernando. I realized it might be the last time I would lie in bed with him. It was possible he wouldn't make it through the night. I was lying on my side, my hand on his arm. Tears were sliding over the bridge of my nose and into my ear, which reminded me of being a little girl. The sun was streaming in through the window, and I was listening to him breathe. I could hear other people in the house, family members. I thought, I'm just going to lie here and pretend I'm asleep. I'm not going to share him with anyone today. They can come in and say what they want, but I'm going to stay here.

I wanted to scoot even closer to him and throw my leg over his legs and my arm over his chest and put my head on his shoulder, which was how I always fell asleep. But I was lying on the wrong side of him, and he was so swollen with fluids I was afraid I would hurt him.

Yesterday morning I looked up from an article at the breakfast table and wished I could read it to Fernando. What I miss most is his physical presence: touching him, feeling him touch me, kissing, sex—we always had great sex. But I also miss our conversations, our walks, those long Sunday-morning discussions we used to have about fate or politics or something we'd read. He was a much faster reader than I was. He'd say, "Hurry up and read that. I want to talk with you about it." Such a pain in the butt. Is there something wrong with me that I don't seem as bereft as some widows, that I'm handling it so well? That's what everyone says: "You are handling it so well." I know he is dead. I just can't believe we will be separated forever. Whoever wrote, "Till death do us part," didn't know what he was talking about.

I read a few years ago that a mother carries her children's genes. We all know the child carries the mother's genes, but when mothers are tested, their blood also contains their children's genes. And the second child carries some of the first child's genes, and so on. All of this genetic material is circulated through the amniotic fluid in the mother. This means Fernando's genes are inside of me, because I carried both his children. (Actually, three of his children, since there was one miscarriage.) When I say, "I feel as if he is still alive inside me," maybe it's because he is still with me, not only in memory or in spirit, but literally in my blood and in my cells.

Poet Angie Estes writes, "In paradise, / Dante says, we will have only a memory / of having had a memory." As the spirits' memories of this world dissipate, as their ties to us lessen, as their visitations become fewer and farther between, is this when our grief starts to wane? What will still bind us if the grief goes? Are we afraid to stop grieving, because it means we've stopped loving?

Another poet, Aleda Shirley, writes, "my dead / have their own dead to find & so must disperse."

As I write this, Fernando's father is dying in an ICU.

When Fernando's mother died, she waited until everyone had left the house except for his father, and then she said, "I felt something pass through me," and she closed her eyes and took a few breaths and died. I believed Fernando was capable of orchestrating his exit this way. He would go when he was ready.

Fernando died on Monday night. Before he did, he turned in bed and with great effort said, "Beth. I have a place." And that's when I asked him to wait for me. I said it might be years, but it wouldn't seem so long to him. I told him I was happy he had a place and wouldn't go to the gray place. Both our children were in the room with me, so he could see all of us. Sometimes I feel guilty that I didn't give them each time to be alone with him, but it felt right for all of us to be together. I sang him some of the songs I used to sing to the kids when I was putting them to bed. I remember Kathryn putting her hand on my back, and Michael behind her, as if they were giving me their strength so that I could sing without my voice breaking.

I remember putting Fernando's hand over my heart, and my hand over his. I remember him raising his arms so he could breathe. I remember his eyes. He had been asleep all day, but now he was fully awake, and in his gaze I saw all his love, all his faith, everything he wanted to say but couldn't. I felt a part of me rush out to him, as if to comfort him, or to go with him. He looked away. I could see that it was hard for him. When he'd told me I had to let him go, I hadn't realized that he'd been trying to let us go, too.

ANXIOUS ATTACHMENTS

When I was twenty years old, I spent a lot of time crying in a closet. I'd just had Michael and lived with Fernando and two of his younger brothers in a small house just north of the university in Tucson. I cried often and I didn't know why. I was embarrassed about it. One afternoon when I was in the closet, I heard Fernando come home from work. "Where's Beth?" he asked his brothers, and I heard them say, "Oh, she's probably in the closet crying again."

Back then, when Michael was a baby, we didn't know what to call him. His name was Fernando Miguel, which didn't seem to fit him. He was the ugliest baby ever, according to one brother-in-law, and so we ended up calling him Magoo, because when he was first born, before his cheeks filled out, he had a big nose, squinty eyes, and a bald head, and when he rooted, he looked like Mr. Magoo blindly flailing around his cartoon world. Ma-goooo. It's a nice soft name to coo to a baby, no hard edges. We also called him *pelón*, which means "baldy" in Spanish: *pelón, pelón, cabeza de melón*. Baldy, baldy melon-head, a chant my grandsons now love to sing from the backseat as we drive along. "Nana," they ask me, "what was it you used to call Dad when he was a baby?" We also called him Buddha Baby, and we'd rub his round tummy, fat with milk, for good luck. It wasn't until a few years later, when we worked as house parents at a shelter care for abused teenagers, that the nickname Michael stuck. Michael, Michael, Motorcycle, the kids would chant when we walked in.

Michael's delivery had been fairly easy, at least as far as deliveries can go. I woke up with strange pains that seemed to be roughly eight minutes apart. When we woke the brothers-in-law to tell them that we were going to drive to the pay phone to call the doctor, one said, "Oh, it's just the pizza she made for dinner. I've been feeling that way all night, too," but the doctor said, "Get to the hospital right away!" By then the contractions were less than seven minutes apart.

This is a joke we always told about Michael, who is a chef now and who delayed his arrival by ten days: when the food got bad in there, he decided to venture out.

We stopped by the methadone clinic so Fernando could get his dose for the day, even though he worried about making me wait while I was in labor. I understood. It's a long story, and, to me, an old one. Although I'd quit months before getting pregnant, I'd slipped a few times. Once, when Michael was in his thirties, he told me that someone had asked him if he had ever done hard drugs and he'd answered, "Not since I was in utero."

I quit doing drugs, but I didn't look like anybody's mother: skinny, blue jeans and tee shirts, bare feet, long hair. After Michael was born, I spent most of the day in bed holding him so he would sleep, reading old novels, and eating gallons of mint chocolate chip ice cream out of the carton. I rarely washed the dishes or cooked. I had a hard time breast-feeding. I cried in the closet. My mother and younger sister came over and cleaned the house. Fernando's mother and little sisters helped take care of the baby. In the photographs, I'm never smiling.

With Michael, my water had broken right as I opened the doors to step into the emergency room and everyone, hearing the sploosh! turned to look at me. Some-one brought a wheelchair right away. In the labor room, the doctor told the nurses to give me some Demerol even though he knew that I'd done heroin and even though the law said that you can't treat addicts or even ex-addicts with opiates. I loved my doctor for his mercy and understanding. The Demerol allowed me to relax between contractions and I'm sure helped speed my labor along—only seven hours for a first baby who weighed almost nine pounds and had a huge round head. I remember, at one point, hearing another woman screaming, but my nurse told me, "No, honey, you are further along than she is. Some women are just screamers."

I remember feeling like a deer lying in the tall grass. I remember floating up out of my body and seeing myself on the bed.

In the delivery room, they tied my feet in the stirrups and, towards the end, when they decided that the episiotomy wasn't enough and they needed to use for-ceps, the doctor told the nurse to give me gas. I didn't want to lose consciousness because they hadn't allowed Fernando in the delivery room, and I was afraid they would take the baby away from me, and so when the nurse came towards my face with the mask, I pushed her away. I sat up as much as I could and slugged her in the chest. They grabbed my hands. The plastic mask clamped down.

I felt a big wet fish slip out between my thighs. Then I heard him cry. Then I passed out again. Then I was waking up. My hands were tied at my sides, my feet still tied in the stirrups. I felt like a trussed turkey. They were stitching me up, I could feel the tugging of the stitches, but I couldn't feel any pain from the needle. I could hear the baby and when I turned my head, he was hitting the sides of the plastic bed. He was so strong. He was red and crying. They untied my hands and put him in the bed with me, nestled under my arm.

By the time Kathryn was born, only three and a half years later, they allowed Fernando into the delivery room. In fact, as they were wheeling me in, I remember saying to him, "I don't think I want to do this again," and he said, "It's a little late to think of that now."

The labor was more difficult than Michael's, more intermittent. I sometimes think that my mind was actually strong enough to stop or slow the pains. I asked them for Demerol because I thought it would help me relax, as it had with Michael, but they said it would stop the contractions. They believed in natural childbirth at this hospital and so I wondered, what kind of childbirth is unnatural?

I could have sworn the nurse was a girl who hated me in high school. She insisted I couldn't walk around or use the toilet for fear that the baby would drop right out of my vagina. She put me on a bedpan and then left for a long, long time. The doctor insisted on IVs and monitors. This is natural? I wanted to ask. "I'm not high-risk," I said. But the nurse didn't listen. "I had a nine-pound baby three years ago," I said, "with no problems."

They ignored me.

The monitors, which were like a pair of stethoscopes, were strapped around my belly to keep track of the contractions and the baby's heartbeat. At one point, one shifted. According to the machine, the baby's heart had stopped. "Go out there and tell them the baby is dead," I told Fernando.

"It's not dead," he said, "the monitor just isn't working."

"Go out there and tell them the baby is dead," I insisted. "If they're going to make me wear this fucking thing, they should pay attention to it."

He left the room and returned with an older nurse.

"How are you doing?" she asked me.

I pointed at the machine. "What does it say?"

"No," she said, "I asked *you*. How are you feeling?"

My feet were not strapped in stirrups with Kathryn, but at one point, without explaining anything, the doctor, a small woman, started to put a long instrument up my vagina. I had told them: no monitors in the baby's skull. It was a new thing, an electrode on a wire, used to monitor the baby's heartbeat during labor, but I had read it often introduced infection and I was not high-risk and so I'd already told them *No* on that one—just as I had said *No* to the monitors around my belly, *No* to the IV, *No* to lying still in bed. Had they listened to me? *No*. So I gave her swift kick in the chest that knocked her almost all the way back to the wall. "No monitor," I said.

Only then did she explain to me that they wanted to break my water to see if it would speed up my contractions.

(When I told her this story, Kathryn said, "You're lucky they didn't kick you out and say, okay, go ahead, go and have that baby on your own." "If they had given me some Demerol," I told her, "I would have been fine.")

Fernando stood behind me and helped me lean forward to push. He kept telling me to breathe. Sometimes he would hit me on the back, "Breathe!" I could feel the wave of pressure that came from my back and wrapped around, my uterus contracting, but there was none of that feeling that told me to push. With Michael, my body had told me when to push and how hard and for how long, but this time, no. Now that I've heard of epidurals, I think this must be what it's like to try to have a baby with an epidural. The connection between your body and your mind is severed, although in my case, it was natural, my mind was somehow blocking most sensations.

(It is interesting to me now, nearly forty years later, that almost all of the scars on my body run along the base of my neck, thin white lines, and that one of my lessons in life, it seems to me, is to learn how to connect mind and body, to allow myself to feel. Perhaps that is true for anyone who has ever been an addict, the scars remind me.)

"Push now," the doctor would say. "Okay, stop. Okay, don't push, even if you want to." The doctor was showing the intern how to do the episiotomy—"You could cut up this way or you could cut up this way"—I could feel my blood trickling down. As they were cutting, they started gossiping about a party they'd been to the night before. Suddenly, I had to push.

"Don't push," the doctor said.

"Shh," Fernando said, "just breathe!"

But I had to push. The world went yellow, as it always does when I get an adrenaline rush from anger or fear. It is no wonder that Kathryn was born crying, that whenever she was angry when she was small, a red birthmark bloomed on her forehead.

Once, over thirty years later, I saw that doctor's name on a wall. I remembered her. I still hated her. Not only because she wouldn't give me painkillers. Not only because she talked about a party while she showed the intern how to splice my vagina. Not only because she tried to break my water without explaining anything to me. Not only because she wouldn't listen to me. No. Because she made me so furious that when she tried to put my daughter on my chest, I said, "I don't want her. Give her to her father."

I'd felt guilty for years, certain that Kathryn had felt, in her first few minutes of being alive, my anger, and had heard me reject her. It was one of the worst secrets of my life. I couldn't imagine saying it out loud without wanting to cry. Fernando was the only one who knew, and I wasn't sure he had forgiven me.

After he died in 2013, Kathryn was trying to figure out why she felt so abandoned, even though Michael and I were still alive, and so I finally told her the story of her birth. "Your dad was the first one to hold you," I told her, "and when I said, *Give her to her father*, it was because I was so angry, not at you, but at the way I'd been treated. *Sshh*, he'd told me, *she can hear you*. He held you in his arms. *She's beautiful*, he told me."

"Oh," Kathryn said, "that explains a lot. Thank you for finally telling me."

And what I think she meant was this: that even from the moment of her birth, he was the only one who was fully present for her—at least when he wasn't watching TV. He was usually fully present for everyone, which is why people were so drawn to him, while Michael and I were always so self-absorbed. Even as a child, Kathryn used to take my face in her hands and turn it to face her own: "Listen to me. I'm talking to you." And how many times had she said to me about Michael, "He never listens! He never calls! Except when he needs something!"

We were standing outside, in the backyard, looking at the way the setting sun turned the mountains pink, sitting on the wall the way Fernando used to at that time of day. She had gone out there, she was on the phone with Michael, listening to him, and I had followed her after a while to see how he was doing. She and I had been talking about our own grief, turning it over like it was a stone we were polishing together, and now this story was a part of it.

Maybe, the first stone of guilt about being a mother, with each child, was set down in my heart at the moment of their births. I felt already that I could not protect them from the world I was bringing them into. After all, I was not listened to, I had to fight. I did not win, exactly.

Here you are, the world had said, just as I was giving birth, not as powerful as you thought. Do the best you can, but it won't be enough.

Sara, my daughter-in-law says, "Whenever I feel guilty about how I am as a mother, all I have to do is talk to you. You always make me feel better."

True. I often lost my temper, especially with Michael, and now, when I take care of their sons, I am appalled at some of the things that rise, unbidden, to my tongue. "You're cruisin' for a bruisin'," I said to my grandson one day, not realizing how horrible the threat until I heard it from his perspective. I realized then that I'd often said, "Goddammit, Michael!" as a kind of everyday punctuation when I wanted him to pay attention.

When I first read about Winnicott's theory of "good enough" mothering in Maggie Nelson's *The Argonauts*, I was so relieved: I thought it meant the kind of mother I had been, where you are continually falling short, never have enough patience, say the wrong things, say mean things, spank them sometimes, or are totally distracted.

And it does, in a way. First there is "ordinary devotion," which is actually extraordinary when you think about it, where the mother meets the infant's every need, a cry of hunger, the whimper of discomfort—and even the needs the baby usually could care less about: dirty or wet diapers. Really, hunger is what drives an infant, literal hunger and the hunger to be held, to feel safe.

But then Winnicott says, inevitably, the mother begins to fail. She cannot meet every need right away, but this is okay, because, gradually, the child begins to fill its own needs, which creates resilience and thus a sense of autonomy.

Even though the definition of "good enough" mothering was not exactly what I'd hoped, Winnicott was still countering the cultural expectations of being a "good mother," which were high enough when I was young but seem impossible now where every minute of the child's life is supposed to be monitored and enriched and mothers never lose their patience or swear. Spanking, strictly verboten. No wonder I make Sara feel better.

Not only was I distracted and impatient, barely "good enough," but I also must have been neglectful. I think of all their injuries. Michael, hit in the forehead by an automatic grocery door; looking up to see Michael on the high dive at the pool; looking down to see Michael's wide-open eyes as he looked up at me through the pool water, how long it took me to realize he couldn't breathe; Michael falling off the pool table in the shelter care where we worked when he was a toddler; Michael falling down a full flight of wooden stairs in the shelter care, his head going thunk thunk thunk on the uncarpeted wood until the final thunk when he came to rest in the threshold. "Michael," I leaned over him, "Michael." I was afraid to touch him in case he'd broken something in his back or neck. And then he started crying. Michael being pulled out of the street from in front of a speeding truck by the long arm of my brother-in-law. I swear his arm stretched like rubber, and all I could do was scream "No," my voice, so guttural, so raw that I could see the rings of sound widening in the air, slowing time.

Although she was always falling off of furniture and shelving because she was a climber, Kathryn didn't have nearly as many close calls as Michael. In fact, other than a perpetually busted lip from falling onto the tile floor, I don't think Kathryn ever had a close call.

And I didn't cry in the closet after I had Kathryn. Maybe I was stronger by then or maybe my hormones were not careening so wildly or maybe, because Fernando and I were having a hard time in our marriage, my depression was more likely to erupt in anger and that anger was directed at him. After all, by then, I had done the training to be a counselor, and I knew that depression was anger turned inward.

With Michael, people had explained to me that I had post-partum blues. They said I was sad because I was no longer pregnant, which I interpreted as meaning I wanted the baby inside of me again. But the explanation didn't make sense. I didn't want to be pregnant again. I hadn't especially liked being pregnant. He had weighed almost nine pounds at birth, I had been slender before I got pregnant, and I was tired of carrying him around inside me.

Anyway, who would want the baby back inside? When you're pregnant, the baby isn't such a distraction. He's just there, a part of you. He doesn't cause problems other than a little indigestion, maybe, a little difficulty breathing. You don't have to change your life much for him, except you can't eat raw oysters or have more than one cocktail or ride horses. Or, in my case, smoke cigarettes or shoot heroin.

But when he's born? Suddenly he requires all of your attention. The baby wanted to breastfeed every two hours. And then he had to have his diapers changed and then I had to wash his diapers and hang them on the line and take them down and fold them and put them back on him. I used to think if I could get four hours of sleep in a row I would be a new person. But who would that person be? Someone who had another child, went back to school, became a writer and a teacher? Or someone who cried in a closet and went back to drugs?

A few years after Fernando died, I started seeing a therapist because I couldn't make up my mind about what to do next. Each of my children wanted me to move to the town where they lived, but I wasn't sure I wanted to. It was the first time in my life that I didn't know what I wanted, where I didn't have a vision of my own future happiness. I thought maybe I was experiencing complicated grief, which can happen when you lose someone after forty years. The therapist explained to me that there are two major anxieties. One is separation anxiety and one is its opposite, encroachment anxiety, and we all feel both of them but to different extents.

This made sense. What had sent me into the closet when Michael was an infant was encroachment, not separation. Of course, there was also the mystery of separation. I remember looking at his face and thinking, where did you come from? Who are you? Maybe that's why we spend so much time gazing into our infants' eyes: You were inside me? We can't figure it out, the mystery of their births, even though we were there. How they did they go from being inside to being outside? How can they be separate people?

When Michael was an infant, we lived in a small, square house. My mother, a realtor, had used her commission to fund our down payment. Two bedrooms, one bathroom, and termites. I often found the brown lines of their dirt hanging in the doorjambs or in the closet, which made everything feel insubstantial. Fernando and I were sure we could hear them munching inside the walls at night. We joked that one push on the western wall and it would fall out of the house. Who knows how old the house was? Maybe it had been built in the 40s or the 50s. There was a stipulation on the mortgage papers that only white people could own it and live in it—no Mexicans, Indians, Jews, or Negroes. (I think this is also when I first heard the word miscegenation.) When I pointed that stipulation out at the closing, I was told not to worry about it, but I wanted it struck from the papers. I was told, again, not to worry. No one enforced it any longer. I felt like the loan officer was patting my pretty little head. In what must have been an unconscious gesture, I signed my maiden name on all the dotted lines and so the papers were not binding and had to be reprinted. The second time we signed, those stipulations had black lines drawn through them. Good thing because that house was often full of Mexicans, Mexican Americans, really, although no one in Fernando's family used that term then.

For the first week or so, maybe, we lived there alone. I could wander around the house all day, soaking in the silence, lost in my own thoughts. Until then, we had been living in his mother's house, twelve people in a small four-bedroom tract home, a continual cacophony of television and voices and the tinny transistor radio his sisters listened to in their bedroom, noise from traffic on the freeway behind the house, jet liners overhead. For the six or seven months that we lived there, I remember loving everything about it: his sisters, who ranged in age from three to eighteen, and the way we all pitched in to clean and mop and do laundry in the old ringer washer that had no ringer on the back porch; his mother's stories and learning to make tortillas and tamales and exotic salads with cucumbers and oranges; his aunts coming over some mornings for coffee, the way we could linger at the table for hours, Spanish words peppering the conversation; the way everything meant something, even your dreams, even a dropped fork, a double yolk in the egg, the way you salted your food. I loved taking the round belching bus through the neighborhoods as I went to and from work, seeing the brightly painted storefronts and hearing Spanish all around me. I even loved the oppressive heat in the summer afternoons, how we waited for the monsoon clouds to build and then, when the thunder and lightning hit and the lights went out, how we'd sit in the darkened living room and listen to more of his mother's stories. Afterwards, we'd emerge from the dark house and the rain would have washed all the dust and heat away and the western sky over the freeway would be a bruised-blue, then mauve, then pink, then streaked with orange and gold light.

As much as I had loved all of that, I also loved the sudden silence of living in our own small house, the big square windows full of light and trees and the distant mountains. Being alone. Hearing birds. Memorizing how the light shifted. Reading novels. Making bread. I had always been rather solitary, I guess, having lived in a 5,000-square-foot house with only my parents and a younger sister. Being alone and silent seemed normal, but I hadn't realized it was my default mode until then, until I saw that, when Fernando came home from work, he would turn on the radio in the kitchen and then the TV in the living room, and then he'd walk down to the bedroom and try to take a nap. I was perplexed. Why did he want those things on if he wasn't going to pay any attention? Why did I have to listen to them? But, then, one of the first afternoons his brothers and sisters visited us, we were all in the living room, talking, maybe watching TV, or maybe not watching it, but certainly it was on, and we looked around and someone said, "Where's Ferdy?" We walked down the hall together and stood in the doorway. He was asleep on the bed in our room, the door wide open, the first time he'd been able to take a nap since we'd moved in. He had needed the crush of their noise and their presence in the house to fall asleep.

When I think of the push and pull of encroachment and separation now, it makes sense to me that my favorite teaching is in residency situations, where, for ten days, you live with your students and the other teachers. For twelve to fourteen hours a day, every day, you prepare and eat meals together and clean up afterwards, you go for walks together, you meditate together, you read the students' work and meet with them individually and in classes, you have intense conversations about books and art, you listen to others read aloud from their work, you sit in front of a fire together at night, you have a karaoke dance party on the last night where only the women dance, and then, on the last day, you stand in a circle around two students who have practiced an a cappella duet and sing for you as a parting gift. And then you go home. And sleep in a room by yourself for days.

I don't think Fernando ever had encroachment anxiety. After all, for much of his early life, he'd lived in various one- or two-bedroom apartments with up to eight younger brothers and sisters. His parents had slept in the living room. In an article I read recently on post-traumatic stress disorder, the author notes that only in the last one hundred years or so have humans had their own bedrooms or slept with only their partners and, only in Western Europe and the States, have children been expected to sleep alone. This is why they bond with their stuffed animals, the writer says.

My therapist, who was born in Italy, said Italians are much more likely to have separation anxiety than encroachment. She said when she wanted to go across town and stay at a friend's house, her mother would ask, Why do you have to go so far away? When we would visit Fernando's parents—or really any of our relatives on that side of the family—we'd have to announce that we were going to leave at least an hour before we actually planned on leaving. "Well," we'd finally say, sitting at the table, "we have to go soon!" A half an hour later, we'd be standing up, around the table, still talking. Fifteen minutes later, everyone might actually have made it to the front door where the first goodbyes and hugs took place. Then some time on the front porch, saying goodbye again, and more minutes down the short driveway to the car where, depending on how hot it was outside, you might spend another ten minutes getting into the car and saying goodbye again and waving, turning in your seat as the car rolled slowly down the street to wave out of the open windows. All of this when we lived only thirty minutes away by car.

After Fernando died, I noticed that when I talked to my kids on the phone, we would say goodbye to each other at least three or four times before finally hanging up. After Fernando died, my therapist said, "You don't have to worry about it so much. Encroachment or separation. Just step back and look at it from a distance. Be amused." After Fernando died, I wondered: if it was true that you had only one life, why would you want to live it far away from the people you loved most?

When we lived in that small house on Blacklidge where Michael was born, there was only a short time, maybe a few weeks, where we were alone. First, a younger sister lived with us so I could send her to the neighbor's house to use the phone in case I went into labor while he was at work. Then, as I got closer to full-term, Sylvia went back home and their brother Geno moved in so he could drive me to the hospital if I went into labor—Fernando worked construction, so there was no way to reach him on the job. Because Geno was only fifteen, he and I practiced driving. Just in case. We also painted the kitchen and played tennis to try to speed up the process. Then, even though Geno stayed, another brother moved in because he was on the outs with his girlfriend. In the winter, because the furnace was so out-of-date, a kind of boiler contraption I still have nightmares about, we all pulled our mattresses into the living room and slept in front of the fireplace. We had strung clotheslines from one corner of the room to another and Michael's diapers hung over us to dry while we slept. In other words, Michael was born into a communal family. There was always someone to hold him. He loved being the center of attention, something that is true to this day. Fernando and I never lived alone, just the two of us, until the year 2000, twenty-six years after we married.

Soon after we'd moved into the house on Blacklidge, Fernando wrenched his back at work when he and a coworker were lifting a 250-pound air-compressor out of the back of a truck and his coworker dropped his side of it. Because his boss didn't file the necessary papers, Fernando did not qualify for disability or even unemployment insurance, so we went on Aid for Dependent Children, AFDC, or welfare. We got around $200 a month because we had one child. Our mortgage payment was $150 a month, maybe a little less. We got food stamps. I remember that after everything was added up, the mortgage payment, gas, electricity, water, the cost of our food stamps, we had $4 left at the end of the month. There was no money for gasoline for the car. We used bus tokens. We must have bought pop because we cashed in the bottles and bought books at the used bookstore. We didn't have a washing machine and so I tried to wash the diapers in the bathtub or we sold our books back and took the diapers to the laundromat. I remember the welfare worker telling me we had $4 "extra" at the end of the month and I said, "Well, yes, but I need to buy soap and toilet paper and do laundry."

She decided to raise the amount we had to pay for food stamps. Then there was $0 extra. Maybe it was because we were allotted only so much for rent and our mortgage payment was higher than that.

At one point, she asked, "And your husband is the father of your baby?"

And I said, "Yes."

And she asked, "How did that happen?"

And I said, "How do you think?"

I realized then that she had some strange assumptions, but I wasn't sure what they were. Maybe it was because Fernando was Mexican and I was white. Maybe it was because I had long hair and wore bellbottoms. Maybe it was because she knew that his brothers lived with us and so she thought they must have been giving us money and we didn't claim it.

"If we come over," she said, "you had better have separate cupboards for their food and yours."

But this was crazy because we were in a recession. There was no work. No one was working in construction and so his brothers did not, could not, contribute, and so I fed all of us on the food stamps allotted for two of us and, when one brother brought friends home with him for dinner, as he often did, and I would say, we don't have enough food for them, Fernando would say, "Then give them mine. Open a can of beans. Make some rice."

His mother had never turned anyone away, he said, not even hobos off the trains who had often begged at their back door. If all she had was a crust of bread or a piece of tortilla, she would give it to them. It was because, Fernando explained, you never knew when one of them might be the Savior. I could imagine her telling him that when he was little but, really, I think it was because she knew what it felt like to be hungry. Her family had lived in a tent during the Depression and two of her younger brothers had died from drinking bad milk.

They would come and check our cupboards? This was my education in what it feels like to be poor. I was sure she disliked me, but I wasn't sure why. Maybe she could sense my privilege, because, by then, I'd gone back to school and was taking classes at the university, and Fernando was taking counseling classes at the Community College, and she thought at least one of us should have been working, and maybe one of us should have been. How did we afford tuition? I remember my grandmother paying mine, which was $250 a semester—I certainly did not claim that—and I'm not sure how we paid Fernando's, which was much less than mine, maybe some kind of waiver because his GED scores were so high or a rehabilitation grant for recovering addicts. I remember turning the oven on and typing my papers in the kitchen until three or four in the morning while everyone else slept in the living room in front of the fireplace. I remember that I had only one pair of socks and Michael used to hide them before I went to class. I remember the humiliation of welfare. I had never experienced anything like that before but, Fernando, for most of his life, had been treated by the white world as "less than" and the way he had always maintained his own self-respect was through hard work. Work is what defined him as a man. And this is why, when the teacher of his Social Work class asked if we would want to apply to be house parents for a shelter care for runaway teenagers, we said, Yes. Of course. Yes. $6,000 a year plus room and board.

I remember telling the caseworker that we no longer would be needing the money, and she was so surprised. "This almost never happens," she said, as if congratulating us on being such a success story, but I still could not forgive her for begrudging us soap and toilet paper.

Soap and toilet paper and bus tokens. How much of the crush of poverty comes from simple things? From not being able to see your way out? I remember talking to my sister-in-law, once, and telling her, I knew it wasn't going to be permanent and so I could bear it. I always knew we would find our way out—although I didn't know it would take at least fifteen years and two masters programs before I got a steady teaching job at the university.

My sister-in-law said, "That's the difference. You knew it wasn't inevitable. When we were little, we just thought it's the way it was. Everyone we saw around us, we were all poor even though everyone's father worked, sometimes six or seven days a week. Everyone's mother made tortillas and had a pot of beans on the stove, and everyone's family had a garden, and every family lived in an apartment or a house that was too small. We were all poor and our families had always been poor and, as far as we knew, always would be. But at least we were all in it together."

For much of my life, encroachment had been my anxiety. Being needed too much by too many people. I felt this when my children were small and their needs were constant, when I taught and felt teaching asked too much of my thinking time, and, later, when I took care of my aunt and then my mother. I often felt like I couldn't breathe. I had an image of myself as being stuck in the center of this big sticky web. When would I ever be free?

But then Fernando died.

With death, there is no separation anxiety. Oh, maybe there is when you hear the diagnosis, but not with the death. For one thing, anxiety is always about the future, what you're afraid might happen. But when you know death is inevitable or when it's already happened, there's no anxiety.

In some ways, it's the same with death as with giving birth: you have to redefine yourself in light of another person. Only, instead of wondering, Where did you come from, you wonder, Where did you go?

For another thing, the separation is just as mysterious. I knew Fernando was dead. I had been in the room as he was dying. I had talked to him, I'd sung to him. But I hadn't realized dying was the end. I hadn't thought beyond getting both of us, and our children, through that moment.

That moment: when what has always been invisible disappears.

You are left with the body, but the body is not him.

For four or five months after he died, our niece, Alicia, who had lost her mother to lymphoma seven years earlier, and Kathryn, who had just finished nursing school, lived with me at the house. Kathryn slept with me for those months. I had always slept close to Fernando. I didn't know how to fall asleep without him. I'd sometimes put my arm around Kathryn's waist. It was winter. I was cold. But then we would have to turn over and fall asleep separately.

After Kathryn had to leave for a job, and I had to sleep alone, I would hear voices as soon as I put my head on the pillow. At first, I thought it was the neighbors standing in their yard, but it wasn't. It sounded like voices on a radio or on an old-fashioned party line, but I couldn't make out what they were saying. I'd listen intently. Sometimes it sounded like other languages. I wondered if I was overhearing the voices he was hearing wherever he was. I wondered if there was a message. I wondered if I was having a psychotic break.

For a while, his spirit was everywhere at once. The slightest breeze was his breath on my neck. If the microwave malfunctioned or if I saw a hawk, he was sending me a message. He was a constant presence in a way he never had been in life. In life, he had come home in the evenings and we'd taken care of the kids or, later, after they were grown, we'd shared a walk, dinner, a bed, but the days were mine. In life, there had always been a space between us, but now he had moved inside. The encroachment was complete. Death had not parted us.

But, and this is the paradox: because he was everywhere, he was nowhere. I began to miss him, even his spiritual presence. I knew he wasn't in the house. I couldn't feel his breath, I couldn't feel him watching me, I couldn't feel him hearing my thoughts. Where are you? I'd wonder. But I knew. He'd gone on, now, without me, to wherever the next place is.

WATER IN THE DESERT

[To] look over this raven land and know the truth—that there is immeasurable water tucked and hidden and cared for by bowls of rock. . .—is by far a greater pleasure and mystery than to think of it as dry and senseless as wadded newspaper. It is not only drought that makes this a desert; it is all the water that cannot be seen.

Craig Childs, *The Secret Knowledge of Water*

On the way home from the doctor, after the initial diagnosis, Fernando had asked me if I was okay. I wasn't. I wanted him to stay home with me, but instead he dropped me off at the house, where I tried to grade papers while he went back to work. Later, as we were falling asleep, he said that all afternoon, when a customer would say, "Thank you," or "Have a nice day," he'd think, "I have cancer."

As a girl, I learned from my mother, who had lost her first husband in the Korean War, to encyst sorrow and bury it deep within, so this is not an essay about grief. It is an essay about water.

In 1977, when Fernando and I had been married for almost four years, we bought a house from a Mormon family on the north side of Tucson near the freeway and train tracks. The first winter it rained so hard that the water rose and began spilling in under the doors. The suddenly lush ivy on the front of our house crawled into the gaps between the window frames and the burnt-adobe bricks. The roof began to leak. Fernando used an ice pick to poke holes in each room's ceiling, so the water would drain into the hole. Then he used duct tape to fasten a plastic bowl over each leak to catch the rainwater. Bowls were hanging from nearly every ceiling; it was easier than moving all the furniture. In the kitchen, we just let the water drip into a five-gallon paint bucket. All day, while taking care of our two children, I heard the water's rhythmic drip. But sometimes I'd forget to empty and refasten a bowl to the ceiling. One night, the bowl over our bed got so swollen with rain that it tipped over, soaking us, and our baby, and waking her up.

The neighborhood was called Flowing Wells, but we came to call it Seeping Sewers because, when the wind shifted, we could smell the fumes from the ponds at the sewage treatment plant. In the middle of the night, we could hear the trains and, maybe because we had small children, I would wake up worrying about derailments and toxic spills. I was not religious, but I had an apocalyptic imagination. I grew a garden in the backyard because I wanted to be able to feed my family when civilization ended.

One fourth of the yard was planted with corn and pinto beans, the wire fence secured by rebar with upside-down Coors cans glinting in the sun to keep the birds at bay. The grapes tumbled down from the arbor over the vegetable plot, the tomatoes sometimes boiled in their skins before I could pick them, and the neighbors shuttered their windows when they saw me approaching with yet more gigantic zucchinis in my arms. We had peach trees, their limbs so heavy with fruit that they sometimes broke in the summer storms. Because our backyard had once been part of a dairy farm, the soil was dark and loamy, and when the children dug to China, as children do, they found old glass milk bottles.

I wasn't very clear on logistics in my apocalyptic imaginings, although I now realize they had something to do with a fear of scarcity inherited from my mother. I had children to feed. What would I do if conditions changed to such an extent that I couldn't feed them? How would I keep neighbors out of my gardens, especially since I'd already shared my zucchini and chard? How would I be able to deny them food for their hungry children? And where did I think the water to keep the garden growing would come from? This was the desert. I was the daughter of a geologist. I knew the water was pumped from artesian wells deep beneath the surface of the earth.

I had the idea, back then, that the world would end in fire or water. In the summer of 2015, two years after Fernando's death, the Catalina Mountains, which rise above the house where we moved twenty years ago, are on fire.

From all of Tucson, you can see the fire at night. The ridge above us glows red, just as it did that first summer, when Fernando told me not to worry because the houses between our place and the ridge were worth more than ours. He said, "The firemen won't let the rich people's houses burn. They'll put it out before it gets to us." That summer, we watched as helicopters dropped an orange fire retardant that contains fertilizers to help the vegetation grow back. This summer they're letting it burn, 150 acres so far, practically nothing when you consider that 1.1 million acres of the American West are on fire and that 5 million acres have already burned in Alaska and 7.2 million in Canada.

I called my daughter and asked her: "If I have to evacuate, what should I save from the house?" "Dad's ashes," she replied. The copper urn was my first choice, too, though it struck me as odd. Not only was Fernando already ashes, but where else would he want his ashes to stay but here, on this small plot of desert near the mountains?

~ ~

For love is strong as death, says the *Song of Songs,*
Many waters cannot quench love, neither can the floods drown it.

~ ~

"When we got water from the tap, it effervesced in the glass," Fernando told me. He was talking about the water at his parents' house in Mission Manor, a new subdivision on Tucson's south side where his family had moved in 1972. "And sometimes there would be a rainbow lying on the surface of the water. When we called the builder, he told us it was because it was a new house. He told us to keep the water running, to clear out the pipes."

When Fernando talked about TCE, or trichloroethylene, I imagined dark plumes spreading underneath the ground. On maps, TCE looks like a big purple feather. From 1952 until the early '80s, workers at Hughes Aircraft and Tucson International Airport used TCE, an industrial solvent, to clean greasy metal parts of airplanes. They later disposed of the spent solvent by pouring it into open pits, directly on the ground or into culverts, where it eventually percolated into the area's artesian wells.

My father had told me that the Tucson basin was like a big bathtub filled with gravel and surrounded by mountains. When it rained, he said, the water seeped through the gravel to the bottom of the bathtub where it stayed for eons—ancient water from the run-off of ancient rains. If you tasted it, it would probably seem brackish.

I was fourteen when my family first moved to Tucson from Colorado in 1968, and I remember standing at the living room window in my parents' house, watching the rain. No one else was home. It was the first time I'd seen the monsoons, the heavy summer rains. The winds were hurricane force, I heard on the radio. The lightning was spectacular and the water was pounding down from the sky, sheeting across the windows. I couldn't see even to the middle of the driveway. I didn't know where my parents and my younger sister were.

If they drop a bomb, I thought, the electricity will disappear and the pumps stop pumping, and suddenly, we'll all be out of water. They warned us in school that Tucson was, after all, a town ringed by missiles, tenth on the list of the top targets of our enemies. The desert, back then, seemed to me an alien landscape, full of plants with thorns and spikes, cacti that resembled swords. I felt I had landed on an inhospitable planet, one where it could easily hit over 100 degrees, day after day, for months on end. If there was no water, I knew, we'd all be dead in three days.

In 1972, just before Fernando and I started dating, his family had moved into the tract house in Mission Manor. It lay smack in the middle of the TCE plume, along the flight path to the airport. He had eight younger brothers and sisters. I remember playing ball with the youngest of them in the front yard. We could hear the planes before we saw them emerge above the roofline. They flew so low that they rattled the windows. Then we saw their white shark underbellies—so enormous, the landing gear, their wide wings. It seemed as if they barely cleared the house, as if we should duck. When we were first married, and I moved in with his family, I often dreamed of planes.

After his family had lived there for a decade or so, people in the neighborhood started dying. Clear patterns didn't emerge, but sometimes several people in one family would die. Finally, the city tested the water. Some estimates showed TCE contamination at 1,000 times the federal health standards. They closed wells. There were court cases. Redlines were drawn around the housing developments, housing developments where 75 percent of the residents were Hispanic and low-income; once the developments were redlined, it was impossible to sell those houses, so people stayed where they were. The cleanup began, but it was already too late. On Evelina Street alone, near the school Fernando's siblings attended, near Mission Manor Park where they played, and near the swimming pool where they swam in the summers, thirty-four cancer cases were documented. Several families now have only one surviving member.

~ ~

My beloved spake, and said unto me,
Rise up, my love, my fair one, and come away.

For, lo, the winter is past, the rain is over and gone;
The flowers appear on the earth; the time of the singing of birds is come.
The fig tree putteth forth her green figs,
and the vines with the tender grapes give a good smell.

The Song of Songs, my literature professor had said in a class I was taking at the time, is one of the few books in the Bible that might have been written by a woman. Since then, I've read that other scholars think it may have originally been a love song or a wedding song from Egypt.

Let him kiss me with the kisses of his mouth: for thy love is better than wine.

A love song to the garden as much as to the beloved.

~ ~

You don't have to drink TCE or ingest it. Even if you drank bottled water, TCE would enter your system through your skin when you bathed. When Fernando's brother Eugene first saw a doctor for hemochromatosis, he told the doctor that he had lived in the area of Tucson that was affected by TCE. The doctor said that hemochromatosis was so rare that a person would have to have complete exposure for that to happen, like falling into a vat of chemicals. "I did have complete exposure," Eugene said, "I bathed in it for decades."

Eventually, they found a tumor growing on Eugene's liver. He had a liver transplant.

TCE is a Volatile Organic Compound, my friend, an environmental engineer, told me. "TCE wants to rise," she said. "It wants to be in the air instead of the water." TCE enters your body when you drink water contaminated with it, but also when you breathe its vapors in the air, especially if you have an evaporative cooler in your home. TCE also enters your body through your skin, especially if you have cracks or abrasions or cuts. The first exposure to TCE, and the first drink of that water, initiates a metabolic process that can result in lymphoma, leukemia, multiple myeloma, and kidney and liver cancers. TCE is thought to act as an accelerant. In other words, if you have a predisposition to a form of cancer, let's say liver cancer, TCE increases your likelihood of developing that cancer, although it may not manifest for decades.

The permissible level of TCE contamination, according to the University of Arizona School of Pharmacy, is less than the equivalent of 2.5 teaspoons poured into an Olympic-sized pool.

"In the word ecology, the root 'eco' is the Greek word for home. It's really about how we manage our home," said Robert F. Kennedy Jr. in an interview with *Grist* in 2004. Responding to a question about environmental justice, he asserted, "In terms of the conventional way that we think of civil rights, the burden of environmental injury always falls on the backs of the poorest people. Four out of every five toxic-waste dumps in America is in a black neighborhood . . . [T]he poor are shouldering the burden for pollution-based prosperity by large corporations who have control of the political process."

Fernando used to describe how his grandmother grew rows of corn and hollyhocks in her garden. He and his brothers would chase one another up and down the rows. She'd hang the laundry in the garden and had a wood stove under a *ramada* and a pot of beans on the stove. She made tortillas there, under the *ramada*, on summer mornings, when it was still cool but before the afternoon rains came. Her tortillas were the big ones, so thin they were almost translucent. There, in the trees, she'd hang terra cotta pots filled with water. The water was always cool, he said, and tasted of the clay.

~ ~

My beloved is gone down into his garden, to the beds of spices,
to feed in the gardens, and to gather lilies.
I am my beloved's, and my beloved is mine: he feedeth among the lilies.

~ ~

When the kids were young, Fernando and I used to take them to the air shows out at Davis-Monthan Air Force Base or drive them out to the "Boneyard," so we could look at all the old planes that had been retired there. There were thousands of them, with sleek or fat bodies and wings stretched like tails behind them. Some had eyes and mouths painted on them. Some were named after American Indians: Seminole, Iroquois, Sioux. Others were called Skydancer and Starship. There was Avenger, Voodoo, Banshee, and Demon, as if the names could give them a magical invincibility. There were also the innocuously named C-123s, which had dropped Agents Orange, Blue, Purple, Pink, Green, and White over Vietnam, Laos, and parts of Cambodia during the Vietnam War in order to defoliate the jungle and destroy crops. From 1962 to 1971, during Operation Ranch Hand, according to the *New York Times*, the US dropped 20 million gallons of herbicides and defoliates and other dioxins, destroying 5 million acres. Some members of the Ranch Hand team revised Smokey the Bear's motto to say *Only You Can Prevent a Forest.*

Still, Fernando loved the Phantom II, its sleek, supersonic lines, its technological beauty. He had always fantasized about space travel. I think he wanted to defy gravity and go out into space, an astronaut far above the dear blue sphere of home.

Fitting, I now think, that it is called the Boneyard. On acres and acres of dirt fields, planes bake in the sun like bones in the desert. Resting there are planes that had strafed tree lines and planes that had sprayed clouds of rainbow herbicides. Before being retired to the Boneyard, those planes were washed clean with solvents, and those solvents seeped into the earth.

~ ~

Let us get up early to the vineyards; let us see if the vines flourish,
whether the tender grapes appear, and the pomegranates bud forth:
there will I give thee my love.

~ ~

Fernando's sister-in-law, who grew up on the south side of town, died of lymphoma when she was only forty years old. She had been tired, but she attributed that to working outside in the summer heat, where she supervised juveniles sentenced to community service like cleaning up the parks or roadways. One day she woke up at two in the morning, worried that she was late for work. She was delirious. Her family took her to the hospital, where doctors sedated her, to find out what was wrong. The cancer had already leached the calcium from her bones; the calcium had gone to her brain and given her dementia. Whenever she woke up, she would yank at the tubes in her arms and say, "Home." They would put her under again. Fernando thought she knew she was dying. For a few years, she had been telling him that she wanted to join the procession to San Xavier Mission at Easter as a *manda*, or a ritual petition, to ask God for a cure for his hepatitis. He told her she should worry about her own health. Maybe he suspected she was ill. She died in 2005 and only seven years later, both he and her brother would be diagnosed with malignant tumors.

When the contamination of the wells first hit the news, the Pima County Director of Health and a few Pima County Supervisors, including Ed Moore, told south side residents in a community meeting at the library that they were getting sick because they smoked too much, drank excessively, had bad diets, and didn't exercise enough. Later, when Moore was asked how he explained the family history of Manuel Herrera, a community activist whose wife, children—all but one—and several grandchildren have had serious and rare illnesses, he again blamed "life-style" habits, saying that the health director had been "scapegoated."

Because TCE did not cause a cluster of like cancers, like childhood leukemia, it was difficult to prove fault, and to hold Hughes Aircraft and Tucson International Airport liable. Attorneys settled with the insurance companies. If a person was part of the original lawsuit, and sick with cancer when the suit was filed, then he or she might have been among the 1,600 residents of a possible 47,000 included in the settlement. On their website, the law firm Baron and Budd's touts this lawsuit as "among the most important litigation in U.S. history involving personal injuries caused by water pollution." The firm says that they hired scientists who proved that TCE caused "several unusual forms of cancer," especially in children, but the results of those studies about cancer, found "at almost epidemic levels" on the south side of Tucson, cannot be revealed because, according to the terms of the settlement, the records of the lawsuit are sealed. This means that none of this evidence can be used to establish precedence in future lawsuits.

The lawsuits, therefore, excluded thousands of potential claimants since such cancers typically do not appear until ten to twenty years after exposure and may not be limited to one generation. *AlterNet*, a journal that focuses on environmental issues, estimated that by 2006, 20,000 had died, become ill, or had been born with birth defects because of their exposure to TCE on Tucson's south side. Yolanda Herrera, who has been involved with the Unified Community Advisory Board (UCAB), a local organization that has fought for citizen's rights on issues of TCE for more than 20 years, told me in a phone interview that it was impossible to know exact numbers since there's been no systematic tracking of the health of those who lived in the area at the time. The Air Force, which contracted with Hughes Aircraft who operated the site in the 1950s through the 1980s, is still in litigation with the city of Tucson. "They want to cut a deal with the city and wash their hands of us," said Herrera, but UCAB is fighting them. "If the Air Force has its way," she continued, "it would hand the city a check," and Tucson would have to continue funding the cleanup of the Superfund site themselves.

~ ~

By night on my bed I sought him whom my soul loveth:
I sought him, but I found him not.
I called him, but he gave me no answer.

~ ~

One of the first dreams I had about Fernando after he died was about water. I dreamed that I was washing his body. I had the huge aluminum bowl, the one that I used to mix *masa* for tamales. It was the same bowl that we put near the bedside when someone felt sick. I had filled it with warm soapy water and dipped the cloth in the water, then rang it out. I washed his face first, just like I had done in the hospital after his surgery. When he closed his eyes, I washed his forehead and eyelids, and then the rest of his face and his mouth and his neck. I ran the cloth down over his arms, which were still strong in the dream, and his wrists, which had always been as thin as mine. I washed his hands, then his chest, still firm from all that hard work, and his stomach, which had more hair than I remembered but not much at all. I washed his penis, and his thighs, which were so white and which also hardly had any hair on them. Finally, I ran the cloth over his calves, which had so much hair that it looked like he had black socks on, and last, his feet. In the dream, it was Fernando's bony feet that I saw most clearly: he had black hairs on his knobby toes. His little sisters used to joke that his feet looked like Jesus's feet and even in the dream I remembered that and knew there was some kind of Christian symbolism going on. But what struck me was that I had not paid more attention to his body while he was alive, for it was his body I missed most.

~ ~

Behold, thou art fair, my love; behold, thou art fair.

~ ~

The liver is a tender and porous organ. Like a sieve, it filters all the toxins from the blood. Any doctor will tell you that although the liver is the one organ that can regenerate itself, you cannot live without it. When you get a virus like hepatitis C or you drink too much alcohol or you're exposed to too many toxins, the liver becomes scarred or fibrous. The sieve gets clogged and so it can no longer filter the blood effectively. Eventually you might get cirrhosis or liver cancer. If the tumors from the cancer are in the lobes of the liver, they can often be ablated or removed. If the liver still starts to fail, you could be eligible for a transplant. But if, like in Fernando's case, the tumor is in your portal vein, the vein that carries 75 percent of your blood to your liver, none of those treatments will work and a transplant is out of the question.

When Fernando's liver started to fail, his abdomen filled with fluid, a condition called ascites. This made him uncomfortable. It was difficult for him to sit without almost arching his back. When they drained the fluid, he said it was the color of coffee. When he ate, he always had indigestion. He felt weak; he was always tired. He said the chemo pills burned the palm of his hand as soon as they touched it. His skin was dry and papery; the whites of his eyes started to turn yellow. Soon, he began to drift, and fall asleep. He could no longer talk, though he seemed largely aware of what was going on. Because his liver could no longer metabolize proteins, the ammonia level in his blood was rising and would eventually go to his brain. Perhaps that was why he could no longer talk, why he drifted. The possibility of dementia from the ammonia scared me more than anything, and I knew it scared him, too. He no longer remembered how to move his legs. The simplest tasks eluded him: how to eat, how to swallow. His legs were as solid as tree trunks, so full of fluid. His kidneys were failing, and there was fluid in his lungs. It was hard for him to breathe. I could tell he knew what was happening, but I hoped he was dreaming anyway, seeing the faces of the people he loved most, and would have to leave. There were things he wanted to say. He raised his arms, trying to breathe.

Fernando wanted the doctors to document the exposure to TCE for his children who drank the water when they visited their relatives, for me, for our relatives who still live on that side of town. Cancer is no longer unusual in families who have lived on the south side of Tucson, even families like Fernando's, with no history of cancer in previous generations. Everyone knows the stories. Still, whenever Fernando would mention TCE to his doctors, they didn't understand what he was talking about. They dismissed his questions. After all, they had their diagnosis: hepatitis C. Exposure to TCE would not change the treatment or prognosis. Fernando understood this. But, he reasoned, because they were scientists, shouldn't they also consider other variables? Weren't they even curious?

But you can't document that which you refuse to see. Or, as they say in Spanish: *No hay nadie tan sordo que él que no escucha.* There is no one so deaf as he who will not listen.

LOS PERDIDOS

My father-in-law was orphaned when he was a child. He came to this country from Mexico, looking for his family and, although he didn't find them, he created his own. He worked on the roofs to support them. Hot-tar roofing, in Arizona, in the summer, is one of the hardest jobs; the temperatures on the roofs can get to 135 degrees. Although he never had even a basic education, he was fluent in two languages and could do complicated geometric equations in his mind. He was curious about everything, and would go to the University of Arizona Medical Center to listen to the public lectures or to Armory Park for the Mariachi Festival. He watched the news programs from Mexico almost obsessively, but he never went back, not even for a visit.

Whenever Fernando watched the news and there were stories about murders or gang violence, he would always say, "Please don't let it be a Mexican." He'd been born in Tucson, and his mother's family was at least fifth-generation: one side had a Spanish Land Grant near what is now Los Angeles and the other side had Yaqui and, probably, other American Indian roots. In other words, the border crossed them; they didn't cross the border. His father had been born in the States, too, in California, although he grew up in Mexico. Still, Fernando self-identified as "Mexican," not "Mexican American," and certainly not "Hispanic" or "Latino" or even "Chicano."

Gloria Anzaldúa explains it best when she writes, "We say *nosotros los mexicanos* (by *mexicanos* we do not mean citizens of Mexico; we do not mean a national identity, but a racial one). We distinguish between *mexicanos del otro lado* and *mexicanos de este lado*. Deep in our hearts we believe that being Mexican has nothing to do with which country one lives in. Being Mexican is a state of soul—not one of mind, not one of citizenship." I didn't really notice this passage in her essay until after Fernando had died, so I'm not sure if he would have agreed, but I think so.

If you ask our children, "What are you?" both, like their father, will answer "Mexican" without even thinking, so deep is their affection for and identification with his side of the family. "Mexican," even though there are times when, like their father, they don't feel "Mexican enough."

When my daughter was about five, she asked me, "Aren't you at least part Mexican? Just a little bit?" I thought about it before I answered, because you shouldn't claim what isn't yours. "I am inside," I told her. "In my heart."

I was always the one who wanted to go to Mexico, to see the museums and Frida Kahlo's house in Mexico City, for instance, and to San Miguel de Allende. Fernando would always tell me it was too dangerous. We had gone once to San Carlos, a small beach town near Hermosillo, with my family when our children were small. I remember when we were at the border, going south, while we were waiting for my parents to get car insurance, some of the Mexican border guards were asking us about our children, if they were both ours. Because Michael was dark and Kathryn light, this was not an uncommon question, especially in the '70s. After all, even though people had intermarried in the borderlands for generations, Arizona had not repealed its anti-miscegenation laws until 1962. No one ever thought Michael was mine and Fernando was always afraid they'd think he had kidnapped Kathryn, so he never went anywhere alone with her. The guards also asked, several times, if we were married, and checked our driver's licenses over and over. Back then, you didn't need a passport and there were no identification papers for children. Their persistent questions made Fernando nervous. Finally, when they walked out of earshot, he said, "Don't talk to them. Your Spanish is so bad, you're going to get the children taken away from us."

In San Carlos, when we drove around up in the hills to look at the beautiful homes of the rich, Fernando kept commenting on all the evidence of backbreaking work, like the roads, which were mosaics made of stones the size of quarters. I had noticed, of course, the families living in abandoned railroad cars by the side of the road all the way down, but not the tires of different sizes on all of the trucks. The poverty that barely registered with my family members deeply disturbed him. His family had been so poor when he was growing up that they often had no water or electricity. He used to go and get buckets of water from the neighbor's hose. His mother used to cook in the fireplace; he did his homework by candlelight. He said that when he turned his work in, the drips of wax humiliated him. Whenever I complained about not having enough money, he would say, "We've never been poor." Or, "I've never let you go hungry." That hunger was the baseline tells you something about his childhood.

Jane Wong speaks of "the poetics of haunting," how stories are not told, how families are haunted by ancestors about whom they know nothing, haunted by the legacy of migration and collective trauma and the silences that surround them. When the past is too painful, who wants to remember? She said when she got a fellowship to go to Hong Kong, her family asked why she would go back to China. Was she crazy? And she said, "The past, these ghosts, they arise." In her practice, in the poetics of haunting, you would go toward the ghosts, the silences, and "rewrite forgotten histories." But the trip to San Carlos was the only time we ever went to Mexico. I wonder now if it was only the poverty that bothered Fernando or if he saw, also, the ghosts of his father's life.

In December of 2014, after both Fernando and his father had died, I went to the state of Guanajuato, because I wanted to see where his father had lived when he was a child. This was a trip Fernando and I had thought of making while he was alive and, although he had trepidation about going to Mexico at all, he was curious about his father's past. He had never met any of his relatives on that side of the family—there weren't even any photographs—and he'd always wondered if any of them were left. When we'd asked his father if he would go with us as our guide, he would sometimes say yes, but more often he would warn us that his ancestor, Pedro de Alvarado, a *conquistador* who came over with Cortez, was still burned in effigy there every spring. Sometimes, especially if he'd been watching too many news programs on the Mexican stations, he would simply say, "Don't go there. Don't have nothing to do with those people."

My father-in-law's family had owned large haciendas in the states of both Guanajuato and Michoacán, which means that they were *hacendados*, the land-owning class that Villa and the Zapatistas had fought against during the Revolution. My father-in-law's grandfather had divided one of the haciendas among his sons, legally deeding parcels to each of them, and so, after the Revolution, he explained to us, the family was able to hang on to the one in Guanajuato. But the other hacienda and its holdings, which were still only in his grandfather's name, were taken away from the family and divided among the *campesinos*.

In *The Labyrinth of Solitude*, Octavio Paz explains that the Revolution was motivated not so much by ideology as by a "hunger for the land," land that, until the Conquest, had belonged to the *campesinos* and allowed them to feed their children. The land reform called for a return to a pre-Conquest form of ownership wherein land was owned communally and not by individuals.

It was a long and violent Revolution, lasting approximately ten years, from 1910 to 1920. In one year alone, 200,000 Mexican soldiers were killed—a number surpassed only by the numbers of those who died in the trenches in World War I during the same period of time. And the violence continued long after the end of the Revolution. All of the leaders of the movement were eventually murdered; one out of ten Mexicans were killed, whole families wiped out.

~ ~

Even though the Revolution ended before my father-in-law was born, Mexico was the site of early trauma for him. When he was five years old, in 1930, someone shot his father in the back and killed him as he was working in the family's trucking firm. Some days later, his maternal grandfather showed up and took his mother and older sister with him, essentially orphaning my father-in-law and leaving him to be raised by his father's family. I know, from my mother-in-law's stories about him, that when he was child, he would hide in the basement of the chapel on the hacienda where they had concealed the statues of Mary and Christ and all of the other religious icons. As he crouched there, he could hear the boots of the *Federales* on the wooden floor above his head. The dirt would sift down as they walked. While his cousins were groomed to become priests and lawyers, he was never allowed to go to school and worked on the hacienda instead as a kind of indentured servant. When he was thirteen, someone shot a horse out from under him and left him for dead.

After that, his uncles dressed him as a woman and smuggled him first to Mexico City to live with some ancient aunts and then, a year later, out of the country, leaving him just on the US side of the border, abandoned again. It was 1939. He spoke very little English, if any. He had the name of his godfather scrawled on a piece of paper, and he went to a market in Olvera Street in Los Angeles hoping to find him. Unfortunately, his *nino* had already died, but the man who owned the butcher shop must have known him because he gave my father-in-law a job and, later, helped him find cousins who were *braceros* working in the fields near Sacramento. Unfortunately, when the authorities moved his cousins to another migrant camp, my father-in-law wasn't allowed to follow them because he was a US citizen. He ended up in San Diego, alone again, driving food out to the Japanese internment camps. In a way, my father-in-law had been in exile since he was fourteen years old and so, by extension, his children would be as well.

I remember asking him once, in the 1980s, while we were watching the news about El Salvador and Nicaragua, what he thought about children carrying automatic weapons. He said he'd carried a rifle when he was a kid in Mexico. He and his friend got in a shoot-out with a *Federale*, perhaps the same one who had killed his father; he couldn't tell who was firing at them because they were hiding behind a rock wall. He said, after the Revolution, when the new government had given the land to the *campesinos*, they often didn't know how to make it produce—but when they did, when the cooperatives were successful, the *campesinos* were then displaced by large companies from the States. "During the Depression," he said, "you could ride out over the land and see men who had rustled cattle to feed their families hanging from trees."

Because of my father-in-law's stories and because the US State Department warned against it, I did not go to Michoacán. In the fall of 2014, while planning my trip with my cousin, Carol, I started reading the news obsessively. I knew, of course, about the "disappearance" in September of the forty-three students from the teachers' college in Iguala, Guerrero, which was near Michoacán, but about 300 miles to the south of where I would be in Guanajuato City and San Miguel de Allende. I knew there were ongoing protests all over Mexico. The day after I purchased our nonrefundable airline tickets to what I thought was a "safe" part of Mexico, I read that one of the top drug lords in the cartels, Hector Beltran Leyva, had been arrested, without a shot being fired, while he ate dinner in a seafood restaurant in San Miguel. Evidently, Beltran Leyva had been laundering some of his drug money by investing in art and opening galleries. I imagined it as a scene out of *The Sopranos*, everyone following the script so as not to harm the tourist trade and scare away the ex-pats and artists.

Because I'd read that you shouldn't travel at night, I arranged the flight very carefully, making sure we would arrive in the city of León in mid-afternoon so that we could make it to the city of Guanajuato before dark. Of course, our plane was delayed, and it was dark when we landed. I must have been very nervous because I kept filling out the Visitor's Permit incorrectly and I kept getting sent to the back of the long line to fill out another. The penultimate time I filled it out, I was sent to the back for using the purple ink I'd been using all along. Ironically, I'd helped the man sitting next to me on the plane, who didn't read either language, fill out his card and he had no problems at all, so I took it a little personally. Was it my last name?

Meanwhile, Carol had struck up an acquaintance with a woman who now lived in LA but was coming back to Mexico for a wedding. Her cousin was picking her up and then they would drive about two hours to the south, to the family's ranch, near both Michoacán and Jalisco, very near where my father-in-law had been raised. When I asked them if they recognized the name, they didn't. When I asked them whether we should stay the night in León, even though we had reservations in Guanajuato, or take the forty-five-minute trip by taxi, they both assured us we should not take a taxi at night, especially not up through the winding hills. I recognized the word *peligroso* many times in her cousin's speech, but it seemed to me to be more in the context of the winding roads and the unreliability of taxi drivers. He never once said the words *bandidos* or *drogas* or *cartels*.

Still, I thought, my children would never forgive me if I got killed in Mexico, especially since their father had died only two years earlier, especially since their *tata* had told me never to go there. Standing in the crush of families in the noisy airport, taxi drivers grabbing at the handles of my luggage, I wondered why I hadn't listened? You never listen, Fernando's voice answered.

Carol, who is as intrepid as she is gregarious, insisted we should take a taxi and so I went to the official line and engaged one to take us to the city of Guanajuato. I perched on the edge of my seat the whole way. The entry into the city through a series of underground tunnels, used previously for mining silver, would have unnerved me had I not already read about them. When the driver deposited us in front of the hotel, I gave him a huge tip both because we were still alive and because he had a long drive back, probably without a fare.

We checked into the Hotel of the Poets, which was built, like many buildings in Guanajuato, into the side of a mountain, and then walked through the narrow winding streets, full of people, to the Plaza San Fernando. It was a small plaza with brightly painted buildings surrounding it, mostly small shops and cafés, the many trees still leafy and green even though it was December. Just a few blocks from our hotel, it would become one of our favorite places to have a glass of wine. That night, it was already dark, probably after 10 p.m., but warm enough to sit at a table outside. The Bossonova Café, behind us, was filled with noisy, laughing diners. We drank our wine and ate our crepes, watching families with their children playing nearby. The *callejoneadas*, student bands dressed as medieval troubadours who gave evening walking tours of the historic sites, paraded through the plaza, playing their guitars and mandolins and singing. At a café at the other end of the plaza, the tables were long and full of people, and the *callejoneadas* lingered there for a while, everyone joining in and singing.

In the following days, as I walked through the streets of Guanajuato, I searched the faces of people in the streets for any resemblance to my father-in-law or to my husband. It was Christmastime, poinsettias and colorful banners were everywhere. On the steep white steps leading up to the university's main doors, law students, mostly women, had graduated and were posing for pictures, their arms full of red roses, their families surrounding them. Both the narrow streets and the wider plazas were crowded and festive, but I saw no one who looked like family. Fernando, like his father, had been tall and looked Spanish. My father-in-law's mother, I'd always heard, was the child of German immigrants to Mexico. I'd assumed they'd come after the First World War but, after his father died, read that many with her maiden name, Curiel, were *Conversos*, Spanish Jews who had escaped the Inquisition first by converting and then by fleeing to Mexico in the 1500s.

The story about how my father-in-law's parents met is romantic. One day, after the *Federales* had burned down a village, his father had seen his mother standing in the rubble and he rode over on his horse, she climbed on the back, and they rode away. They fled to California where they were married and where my father-in-law and his sister were born. After about five years, they returned to Mexico and his father was killed because he was a *Cristero*, one who had sided with the Catholic Church after the Revolution, when the new government adopted anti-clerical policies. But that's about all my father-in-law ever said about his parents. After all, he was only five when his father was killed and his mother abandoned him and it could be that no one had ever told him any other stories. For him, Mexico was never the loved and longed-for motherland. Instead, it was a place of pain, loss, and oppression, a place he taught his family to fear.

Perhaps because of this fear—or maybe just common sense—Fernando would never go to Mexico when we were young and used heroin. He would never go and he never wanted me to go. I went anyway, of course, to Nogales, a border town, and ran small amounts. We would wait until nighttime to cross back over because they were unlikely to have a matron on duty and only a woman could do strip searches of other women. I remember walking up into the dusty hills to the dealer's house, which was a shack, really, and sitting around a table where one of us tested the dope. I remember there was a curtain and, behind the curtain, the sounds of a woman shushing small children. The dealer was nothing like the stereotypes in the movies now. He was barely feeding his children, and he was shielding them, as best he could, from what we were doing around that table. He certainly did not have a big black SUV or a machine gun. He may have had a pistol, but if he did, I never saw it.

I wonder, sometimes, if this is part of my fascination with the cartels, a feeling of guilt for ever having used drugs. We never hurt anyone, unless you consider the fact—which I didn't then, but do now—that being a consumer of drugs creates the market and, without a market, no cartels. There are other sources of more personal guilt, of course. During the three years that I used narcotics, I knew sixteen people who died, either by overdose or by suicide, and I always felt guilty, as if by doing the same drug, I was complicit in their despair—after all, I hadn't had the wherewithal to help them or even notice they needed help.

And I never thought of our actions as being violent, although we were complicit in the violence going on around us. One night, people Fernando and I knew forced their way, armed, into another dealer's house on the south side of Tucson; they robbed him and his wife of their stash and money. Afterwards, the robbers came to the house where we lived with several other people and asked if they could hide their weapons with us for a small share of what they'd stolen. A few hours later, in the middle of the night, we were awakened by helicopters, searchlights trained on the doors, and cops in flak jackets with automatic weapons. I don't remember a warrant, but they came in. We had to stand against a wall while they ransacked the house. We'd outsmarted them by stashing the weapons and our drugs in the trunk of an abandoned car down the street. Angry that they couldn't find anything, they kept us up for hours, taking us one by one into the kitchen to ask us questions about the robbery.

One of the guys, they said, had pointed his gun at the baby's head to make the dealers give up the stash. I didn't know if this was true, but maybe it was. Maybe that's why they'd called the cops. Or maybe they'd hidden the stash in the child's room. I think that is what happened, the child endangered by both sides. I'd like to think that we were shocked by the details of the robbery. Those details, that was not who we were and not who we wanted to be. We quit soon after. I was nineteen and Fernando was twenty-two. Had something happened that night, had someone been killed, we certainly would have been morally complicit and, legally, we would have been accomplices after the fact.

Now that I'm older, it's easy to see how much drug abuse has changed the landscape of our culture. Over the last thirty years I've read so many student essays about parents who have not been able to take care of their own children due to drug and alcohol abuse. I have friends and relatives who are raising their grandchildren because their own children are addicts. One of my graduate students, who is my son's age, recently told me, "I love you. You are who my mother would be if she had ever stopped using drugs."

I know families and communities here have been torn apart both by drug abuse and by the War on Drugs with its high incarceration rate, especially of Hispanic and Black men. But when I think of Mexico and, now, Central America, I feel deep shame at our complicity in their devastation. "Mexico has been suffering, for [over] a decade," Álvaro Enrigue, a Mexican novelist, writes, "the insurrection of a group of bloody capitalist insurgents fighting for their right to sell drugs. Like all Mexicans, I am traumatized by the war, I can't think of anything else [other] than what is destroying a country deliriously beautiful and generous."

Our appetite for drugs is monstrous, all-devouring. The Mexican Cartels make from 19-29 billion dollars a year by selling drugs to us, and at least 200,000 people have been killed since Felipe Calderón, then the president of Mexico, agreed with the Bush administration to cooperate in the War on Drugs.

If only our complicity were limited to creating the market—but it's not. Fifty percent of the guns confiscated in Mexico were first legally purchased in Texas. In 2004, Congress did not renew a ban on the sale of assault weapons, and since then, according to Mexican Ambassador Arturo Sarukhan, these "long weapons" have replaced handguns as the cartels' "artillery of choice."

~ ~

Just days before I arrived in Guanajuato in December of 2014, there had been protests about the recent kidnapping and disappearance of the forty-three students in the state of Guererro. There were banners and signs of protest still hanging throughout the city. The murder of the students—everyone assumed they were dead, although their bodies had not yet been found—was only one example of state sponsored repression in Mexico. The students were from Ayotzinapa, a school of democracy whose teachers, according to scholar Francisco Alonso, had been fighting for more than fifty years against "corrupt policemen, homicidal soldiers, paramilitary forces, *caciques*, and now the narco state." Those students were targeted because Ayotzinapa had provided a disproportionate number of leaders to the state's social movements and, perhaps, because they had disrupted a speech by the mayor's wife on the afternoon they were kidnapped.

Given that history, it was not surprising that in the hills above and around Iguala, when they were searching for the bodies of the students, they found over thirty mass graves, over one hundred and thirty bodies—although none of them belonged to the students—and over three hundred people came forward to say they'd had family members "disappear" in the last ten years. According to *The New York Times*, the mayor and his wife, who ordered the disappearance of the forty-three students, were working with the local drug gang, *los Guerreros Unidos*.

What was surprising was not the massacre. What was surprising was that the students were willing to protest in the first place, that families began to come forward to look for their dead, that protests erupted throughout Mexico, that artists created installations in protest—that people all over Mexico were willing to take the risk of speaking out, given the larger context of violence and silencing in which this atrocity took place.

When I was in Guanajuato, I often walked through the streets imagining it was 1937 and I was a twelve-year-old orphaned boy from a ranch a day's ride away. How steep the hills were, how colorful the buildings climbing them, the trees' foliage trimmed into squares in the central plaza, the plaza filled with families and music and old people sitting on benches. One day, on my way to the plaza, I wandered into a big church. It seemed carved out of gray stone. When I first walked through the doors, there was a large statue of Christ, also carved out of gray stone, carrying the cross, one knee on the ground. His eyes were turned toward heaven or else rolled back in his head from pain. The crown of thorns, the stigmata, the blood dripping. It all felt so heavy, this suffering we are expected to bear in this life; the next life, the eternal life we are promised, seemed so far away. The child in me wanted to escape into the streets noisy with this life.

The only time I was afraid in Guanajuato City was the evening before we left for San Miguel. I needed to get some cash, but all the ATMs had lines that wound around the buildings. Someone, maybe the woman at the hotel, told me to go to the ATM at the hospital. You had to go inside and so not as many people went there, she said. I arrived at the hospital at the same time as the police. Had there been a shoot-out? Were they worried about one? But no. Evidently, they were just going to take the cash out of the ATM and transfer it to the bank. They were there in lieu of an armored vehicle. "*¿Está cerrado?*" I asked, pointing at the machine. They were very courteous and let me withdraw my money before they emptied it, but being surrounded by at least six heavily armed men—we're talking machine guns and side-arms and flak jackets and helmets—made me anxious. I didn't know if it was the safest or the most dangerous withdrawal I had ever made.

The next morning, when we took a taxi to the bus station, the driver asked me why we were visiting Guanajuato. "My father-in-law was from here," I said, "but I am from Tucson." He asked me how I found it. "Beautiful," I said. "And the people?" "*Muy simpatico,*" I said. He told me about his one journey to Arizona and how he had almost died. He had been so relieved when he finally made it to a small town, but there, he had been denied even water. I apologized that my countrymen were not *simpatico*. "*Lo siento,*" I said, "*lo siento mucho.*" And I meant it. My father had always told me that it was illegal in the state of Arizona, as it should be, to deny someone water, but more recently I've heard stories about how the right-wing vigilante groups pour salt into the gallon water jugs left in the desert for border crossers by the Samaritans and other humanitarian groups. Lately, the Border Patrol has been filmed puncturing the water jugs. "My son," the taxi driver said, "went to Toronto five years ago and he already has a good job, a car, a wife, and is buying a house soon. They will have children! Here," he said, "I had to work for over twenty years to buy a house. But at least I am still alive."

Now, when I think of my father-in-law coming alone to the US at the age of fourteen, I wonder how he even managed to survive. I have a twelve-year-old grandson, with skinny arms and smudged glasses, a little younger than my father-in-law would have been when he was shot off the horse and left for dead, when his uncles smuggled him from one part of Mexico to another until it was safe for him to leave the country. How did he make it from the border to LA? Did he hop a train? Did he hitchhike? How long did he live on the streets before finding the butcher who helped him in the market on Olvera Street? Did he go hungry? Was he afraid?

~ ~

After Fernando died, my daughter and niece and I often spent afternoons with my father-in-law. We sometimes talked for hours and then, just as we were about to leave, he would become very emotional. We'd sit back down at the kitchen table and listen as he told us old stories of his early life in Mexico. There is one that I can't remember fully, perhaps because my father-in-law was speaking in both languages. It was a story about a small animal, a donkey or a mule, a baby animal that had its legs bound for some reason, and my father-in-law had to watch it as it struggled and struggled and then it was killed. I can't imagine he had any power over the situation. I can't imagine he could have stopped the torture. He was a child, after all, and there must have been older children or adults around him. But he was leaning forward as he told us, talking softly, his elbows on his knees, his hands shaking when he brushed them across his face in front of us. He felt so guilty. He wished or believed that he could have prevented this animal's suffering and the fact that he hadn't was coming back to haunt him. He told us he played music all night, putting the speakers on either side of his head, hoping to be able to sleep, but he could not dislodge the visitations. He could not forget.

In San Miguel de Allende, my cousin Carol and I walked every morning to a coffee stand down the street from the house where we were staying. We got our coffee and a pastry, if we wanted, a glass of fresh-squeezed orange juice, an order of *huevos revueltos* which, I learned, is how you say scrambled eggs in Spanish. We then sat at one of three small tables in the courtyard, taking our time, planning our day. It was such a sunny, pleasant place, a rock wall on one side and a wall of exposed brick on the other, geraniums, poinsettia, and bougainvillea all blooming in their pots, absolutely spotless white tile on the floor. By then, after only a few weeks in the country, I agreed with the novelist Álvaro Enrigue that Mexico was deliriously beautiful and generous. The young couple who owned the coffee stand told us that they were from Jalisco and had had to leave there because of the violence. His parents had helped them move and start this coffee stand. "We miss home very much," he told us, "but we couldn't raise our daughter there." His wife was pregnant with their second child.

    Although both Guanajuato and San Miguel were free of violence when I was there, the threat of it tinged everything. With every interaction, I could see it in the periphery of my vision. *Not* looking, like not looking at someone's impending death, took its psychological toll. Not looking changes nothing.

One afternoon Carol and I went to *Las Bellas Artes*, which used to be a convent and is now an art institute. There we found the installation, *3000 flores negras por los más de 3000 desparecidos*—"3000 black flowers for the more than 3000 who have disappeared." There were also black and white *del sol* banners decorated with images of Mexico's last three presidents—Fox, Calderón, Peña Nieto—next to banners decorated with skulls. Another installation was a shrine, really, with photographs of all forty-three missing students from Ayotzinapa. Even while we were inside the stone room looking at the photographs, we could hear music, a violin and a guitar. We went outside. The courtyard was lush and green, tall trees, oleander and bougainvillea. There were two students across from us, up on a second-floor balcony, playing the theme song from the 1968 movie, *Romeo and Juliet*: "A rose will bloom, it then will fade. . ." the only lyrics I remembered, although the tune stuck with me for the rest of the evening. We stood in the doorway and listened. We were standing next to a huge papier-mâché skull, white, but covered with drawings and the words, in red, *tienen memoria*: they have memory. The skull, the bones have memory; they would speak if they could.

ORDINARY DEVOTIONS

When my daughter was thirty-six weeks pregnant with twins, she checked into the hospital to deliver even though she was not in labor. Her husband called me in the afternoon and left a message that I should come from work right away: they had decided to do a C-section. I tried to drive carefully. The message didn't say that this was an emergency C-section, but I'd been called out of class, and the hospital was an hour away.

This was the day before Donald Trump was elected. I had recently moved to Oregon from Arizona and so the heavy November sky above the forest seemed out of a fairy tale. The narrow winding roads were possibly slick with black ice. I was afraid deer might leap in front of my car or a semi might veer into my lane.

I was worried about the C-section because it was a change of plans. Just the day before, the doctor had said both boys were head-down; she thought they could try a vaginal birth. The other doctor on call was great, she'd told Kathryn, at reaching up into the uterus and pulling out the second baby. Even breech. I did not like to imagine this happening to my daughter, but neither did I like thinking about a C-section.

That day, as I got into the car to drive to the hospital, everyone thought Hillary Clinton would win. Some predicted by a landslide. My friends were buying champagne. I was not so sure. Disembodied heads, like Trump's—male, blustery, bullying, blind—had been hanging over the landscape for decades. Limbaugh, Gingrich, Cheney, to name a few, now Ryan and Pence, all men who called themselves "pro-life" although they would take food stamps away from the poor, health care from children, and social security from the elderly.

When I got to the hospital, Kathryn was still in her room, waiting. She explained to me that Baby A was still head-down, as he had been ever since she'd gone into premature labor a month earlier, but Baby B was transverse and so the current doctor on call had said, "Call me a wimp, but I'd feel better doing a C-section." Kathryn, who was a nurse and who'd long ago reconciled herself to having these children however she could, agreed. "Nothing about this pregnancy," she told him, "has gone as planned."

When they came for Kathryn, she stood up and walked out of the room, one hand closing the hospital gown behind her. The nurse was by her side, helping her guide the IV on its pole. Kathryn is tall and strong and when her hair is down, it hangs to her waist in dark waves. Her body looked nothing like I remembered mine, so wide and soft mine was. I'd carried low, with blue veins showing through the skin. She carried the babies out front, her belly round and hard, her breasts full. She looked much more like her father's sisters, I thought, although I didn't remember ever having seen them naked. When I put lotion on Kathryn's back after her showers, I'd think about how different our bodies were, about how I'd never seen my own mother's body until she was dying and I was taking care of her, about how my mother had never seen my body naked once I was no longer a child, about how no one had seen me naked since Fernando died. I should remember this moment, I'd tell myself, my daughter's body, pregnant.

That day in the hospital, just before she rounded the corner towards the delivery room, I realized that I'd imagined her on a gurney; I'd imagined kissing her forehead as they wheeled her out. Instead, she was walking away from me. I said, "I love you. I'll see you soon." She gave a small wave with her hand. "Love you."

I told myself: it is nothing. A small operation, that's all. A procedure.

A half an hour later, my son-in-law, Justin, popped his head into the room and said, "Kat's fine! Both boys are healthy!" And then the doctors, pushing one of the babies in a rolling crib, called to him to follow as they raced to the Neo-natal ICU.

I waited. There was something about the election on the TV in the room, but I had muted it.

I remembered when my first grandson had been born eleven years earlier. The same thing had happened. My son had rushed out of the labor/delivery room with the doctors and the baby on their way to the NICU, where the baby, the tiny baby, who had been born at only thirty-one weeks, was going to have to live in a plexiglass crib for six more weeks—until just about the age of these babies, gestationally speaking.

"Stay with Sara!" Michael had called to me. I went into the room and stood next to her, while they prepared to surgically remove the placenta, which had attached itself to her uterine wall with scar tissue. This condition, known as placenta accreta, without intervention, can result in the death of the mother. I didn't know this at the time, but I felt it. I felt she was in danger. Childbirth in this day and age, I thought, in such an advanced country, was not supposed to be so dramatic: a tiny baby, my daughter-in-law at risk.

Now, in this hospital, the day before the election, Kathryn was the only one I was worried about. I didn't even know the babies yet.

Of course, I hadn't known Kathryn when she was first born, nor Michael. They'd been small strangers, their appearance in my arms mysterious even though I'd been present at the moments of their births. I remember gazing at them and wondering who they were. I remember hoping I would love them.

I didn't know then that giving birth to them would make me essential, would attach me to this world as if with scar tissue. Even when Fernando died and some part of me longed to go with him, I would have to stay here. I would have to learn to live with a loneliness that not even my children or my writing or my grandchildren could fill. How had this happened? Death, it seemed to me, was as mysterious as birth.

In so many fairy tales, the mother abandons her children, usually through death, and that was why I had to drive so carefully, not drink too much wine, not mix wine with sleeping pills, etc. My children were not ready to be orphaned, even though they were both adults and were now, both of them, parents themselves and therefore essential—if not to the larger world, then within their own smaller ones.

Of course, as I sat in the room, waiting for my daughter, the irony of my fears did not escape me. I was watching the muted television news, and I was aware of what was *not* being shown: *not* the children actually being orphaned or killed in Aleppo, *not* the families of refugees in flimsy yellow boats on the Mediterranean seas, *not* the child refugees atop the train called The Beast coming up from Central America and Mexico, *not* the children of Flint who had no clean water to drink, *not* the women giving birth in tents as they were protesting the Dakota Pipeline.

Those children were not even blips on our collective TV screen.

Instead, there was this blustery man, his head hanging over the landscape, all puff and noise, like the *Wizard of Oz* before the curtain is opened. He pulls the levers. The show begins. Even if we see through the smoke, we are riveted.

A few minutes later, they wheeled Kathryn in on her bed. Was the baby with her? Or in his own little crib? I can't remember. But I think he was lying on her chest, skin to skin time, they call it, or kangaroo-ing. He must have been lying on her chest because I remember a picture like that, the small baby, only four and a half pounds, lying naked on her chest, the blanket tented over both of them. I was so relieved to see my daughter still alive, her hand stroking her baby's back.

I've always wondered about all the dead mothers in fairy tales. Is this because, back when the tales were written, so many women died in childbirth or is it, simply, because fairy tales often reflect our collective angst? As a child, what could cause you more anxiety than being motherless? But, also, as a mother, how could you bear to leave your children?

When I was thirty-two, I had a tumor on my thyroid gland and for about a month, while I was waiting for surgery and the biopsy, I was afraid I had cancer and was going to die. My children were then eight and twelve and it kept me up nights, my fear of being lost to them. I knew nobody could be as good a mother to them as me and so I bargained with God: Just let me finish raising them. I'll give up everything else. I'll even give up my writing—which, I had to admit, would be impossible, and so I changed my bargain to: I'll give up hope for future publication. I'll give up fame and fortune, which I wanted desperately when I was thirty-two. I'll sacrifice my career for them.

Still, just in case, I picked out their future stepmother, the woman who would become my husband's second wife and replace me. She was the sister of one of my sisters-in-law. Her name was Hilda and she seemed smart and kind (like me) and cheerful (unlike me). Once when Kathryn had been small and I was holding her in the rocking chair, she had been twirling a ringlet of my hair around her finger—I had a perpetual perm in those days—and she had asked me, "If you die, can my new mom have curly hair like yours?" Hilda had naturally curly hair. I remember now that this was a deciding factor. But how would I have put this plan into action? I didn't know. I figured the dead have their ways.

Fernando plus Hilda, (which, in Spanish, is pronounced Heelda): it had a certain ring to it. After the surgery and the biopsy, benign, I'd told Fernando about my plans. He said Hilda would have been a good choice, but he was glad I hadn't died. He told me he had prayed to God to give me some of his time, if necessary.

In Mexican folklore, there is a cave with the candles of our souls. They are all burning. Some are tall, some are not. And even though a tall candle should foretell a long life, Death can blow it out whenever he wants. Death is a capricious fellow.

While Kathryn was pregnant, I would pray: Please, don't take her. I could bear anything but that. But then I would remember my mother telling me that God never gives you more than you can bear, so I would have to amend my prayers because I didn't want to tempt God into proving me wrong in order to show me that I would, in fact, have to bear whatever he gave me as long as I had children or grandchildren who needed me.

Of course, this was my conundrum when Fernando was so sick. *Please please please please,* I would pray, afraid to put my most fervent hopes into words. Lest the opposite happen? Which it did. And the universe was thus proved Godless? No. Oddly enough. It was simply proved mysterious and unyielding, without comfort, except for the comfort we create with and for one another.

That evening in Kathryn's hospital room, as the shift changed, the nurses stood in the corner of the room, one briefing the other. I heard about the T-cut, an inverted T—they'd had to make a second incision, up from the first, through the uterine wall to save Baby B. After Baby A came out, there had been a vacuum and the uterus had clamped down, trapping Baby B up under her ribs. Since they shared a placenta, once Baby A's cord had been cut, Baby B couldn't get any oxygen. He had fluid in his lungs. Amniotic fluid? I looked at Kathryn. She was still so drugged. She turned her face to me and said, "I could feel them pulling on him and pulling on him and pulling on him. I kept talking to Dad, asking him to help us."

Down in the NICU, Baby B was lying face down on a warm bed, tubes in and out of him, helping him breathe. He was so bruised, especially his legs and feet, where they had tried to pull him out. I wanted to touch him, I stroked his back, but he started crying. The alarms went off. The nurse ran in. "His skin is too sensitive," she said. "It's like someone feverish with the flu. If you want to touch him, just place your hand, like this, over the top of his head."

The next day, as the election results came in, Justin kept turning the TV on and off. On, because we were in suspense; off, because, as he said, "We're not watching this." We took a picture of Baby A flipping the bird with his tiny hand. We visited Baby B in the NICU; he now had a CPAP mask over his face, which I found alarming. Kathryn was still vomiting from the medication, holding a plastic bag in one hand and trying to breastfeed Baby A with the other.

Very early the next morning, I had to drive back out to the artist's residency to teach. Unless there was an emergency, because we were allowed to leave only for emergencies, I knew I wouldn't see Kathryn or the babies until the residency was over, in five days, which seemed a long time in the snowy scheme of things.

I wondered what had happened there in my absence, out at the residency near the caldera of an ancient volcano. Before the residency, in anticipation of the election, the university had sent out an email cautioning all faculty not to campaign or advocate for any particular candidate. I had seen many of these warnings in my teaching career in the state of Arizona and thought little of it, but the head of my program interpreted it to mean: no discussion of politics or candidates. At the residency, because we lived with and ate with the graduate students, the boundaries were too blurry, she said. We were on the clock 24/7 and we had to be sensitive about the students' possible fear of being graded adversely if they held opinions different from ours.

There was some discussion about the verb "discuss"—how it differed in meaning and intent from the verbs "campaign" or "advocate," how it might be closer to "analyze," how it might, actually, be our duty as educators to "discuss" or, in the very least, to not shut down a discussion that students might initiate and need to have. We were, after all, teaching adult writers, people who thought and wrote about such things as politics.

The penalty for discussing politics with students? One thousand dollars. I made some quick calculations about how much I had in savings and how many times I would be able to break the rule and whether or not it would be worth the money.

Furthermore, we could not watch election returns with our students. We would have to go to a small town, a half an hour away, and watch the returns in a bar. "What if there are students in the bar," we asked. She wasn't sure. What if there are cowboys who love Trump, (we didn't ask). But, after all, we were only a three-hour drive from Malheur, where the Bundies and their right-wing friends had taken over a bird refuge on federal land. With guns. And some of us were not white and some of us were not straight and some of us were not cis and none of us loved Trump. And none of us packed heat, as they say in the movies.

This discussion filled at least two faculty meetings.

What about if we gathered in one faculty member's room, an A-frame, which was set apart from the dorm rooms, where we could not be heard expressing our opinions?

Yes, she decided, we would have to sequester ourselves.

Yet all of this paled, at least for me, when considered against a T-cut, a doctor cutting through my child's flesh, through her muscle, and a baby, her baby, who might have gone without oxygen, who might have died, I thought, had they opted for the vaginal delivery. Was I being like my mother, I wondered, overly dramatic? But the doctor who had delivered the babies, had said, "There are only three things that scare me about delivering twins, and this is one of them." The babies had been born almost three minutes apart. Did this mean the longest Baby B might have gone without oxygen was three minutes?

One of my former graduate students had lost her baby, her beautiful, full-term baby girl, to oxygen deprivation. The baby survived the delivery, although her brain did not, and she lived for a few months, her parents caring for her while her organs gradually shut down. Another woman had written a book about her experience with the loss of her son due to asphyxia. She chose not to feed him. His organs shut down much more quickly and he died within days. I admired their strength, both of them, but thought I would not be able to deny my child food. To die from starvation, I've read, is very painful.

Back at the residency, in my room, I timed it. Three minutes was a long time. It took me about three seconds to take a breath, but then I could hold it for only thirty seconds before releasing it and needing to take another breath. And, of course, this was an unnatural breathing pattern, not one a baby not-yet-born could master. No wonder he had amniotic fluid in his lungs.

The night before, at the residency, when the election results became clear, several people had needed to take a breath. This is what I'd heard. One had cried out in grief. Many were sick to their stomachs. Even that day, when I arrived, they said some sort of "flu" was going around. Or maybe it was anxiety. I delivered ginger tea to a few people. It was all I could do. Needless to say, there was tension. But in spite of, or maybe because of the tension, because tension does feed art, words were written and arranged in powerful ways, artists' books were made, people cared for one another in ordinary ways, by listening and preparing food.

The first time I saw Kathryn after the residency, she was walking hunched over, her fingers absently stroking her belly as she had done when she was pregnant. She seemed disconnected, almost vacant, and I didn't know how to help her get back into her body. Then my sister came to visit and she held her. She said, just like our mother might have said, "I am so sorry you had to go through that." I watched as Kathryn's face crumpled, the way it had when she was a child and allowed herself to cry.

I often felt like crying when I visited Baby B in the NICU for the morning feedings. One day the NICU nurse tapped him on the forehead and said, "My granddaughter was deprived of oxygen at birth. She's sixteen, but it's been a long haul. You never know what it does to their brains." "My oldest grandson has cerebral palsy, but you'd never know it," I told her, "he's eleven and reads at the high school level." I said this partly to counteract, for the baby's sake, what she had just said.

I wanted to sing to him as I'd sung to my babies, but instead I only hummed: *breathe, breathe, breathe.* Breathe deeply, baby. We love you. You can heal your lungs, baby. You can heal your brain. Brain cells are the only cells in the body that differentiate themselves through use, I hummed to him, which is why one part of the brain can take over for another.

By Thanksgiving, both babies were home and Michael and Sara came to visit with their two sons. My grandsons were playing a computer game in the other room and I kept hearing the older one say, "I'll sacrifice myself for you." I knew it was a game, but it made my heart hurt. Who would want one child to have to sacrifice himself for another?

My son told me he was going to Standing Rock with other people from his church. This was when they were blasting the Water Protectors with water cannons, even though the temperatures were often below freezing and the water could endanger their lives. This was when veterans and people of faith had vowed to go and put their bodies between the cannons and the protestors, when others were shoring up the shelters for the winter, when the authorities ordered an evacuation out of a concern for "public health."

"This is not the first time we have survived winters here," one of the Sioux leaders said. But, of course, it would be the first time with the water cannons, I thought. "I'll sacrifice myself for you," my son's son kept saying, but I did not want my son to stand in front of that wintery assault.

We had relatives who were Sioux and relatives who were Yaqui and, of course, over half of our family was Mexican, although they had been born here, for generations, even when the land was part of New Spain and Mexico. What does it take for us to be considered Americans, my husband used to ask—even though his grandfather had served in WWI and his uncles in WWII, Korea, and Vietnam. My nieces and nephews kept posting on Facebook their fears of the Trump presidency and how it would affect their children. I kept imagining the way the force of the water would bruise Michael's flesh, the ice crystals in his hair, the water in his lungs.

"Don't go," I wanted to say to him even though I knew he and Sara put themselves on the line for social justice all the time because working for social justice is one of the first tenets of their faith. Almost all faiths, all myths, even all fairy tales, are about self-sacrifice for the greater good. One grandson says he will sacrifice himself for the other. He was premature and, even now, at age eleven, has arms like toothpicks. He has painted his fingernails red and wears a safety pin on his shirt even though, in the schoolyard, I've seen his sturdier seven-year-old brother have to stand between him and two bullies.

Faith might help us bear our burdens, I knew, it might help us devote ourselves to others, but it can't change what will happen when flesh meets steel or a wall of freezing water.

As we sat around the table, I thought of the irony of celebrating Thanksgiving while tribal members were coming together and risking their lives in North Dakota, and I realized that only two of us were not Mexican, not Jewish, not gay. In other words, only two of us were white, Anglo-Saxon, Protestant, and straight. Only two of us were not marginalized in some way, not vulnerable to persecution.

The day after Thanksgiving, my daughter and I were holding the babies, their soft bodies yielding against our chests. I remembered this feeling. It was like praying. "What shall I put on their Social Security forms?" she asked me. "Hispanic? Latino? White?"

When I was a young mother, I feared everything. I'd been reading about history and just learned that American Indian children had been forcibly separated from their parents, and so I was afraid there might come a day when someone would try to take my children away from me because I was white and they were brown. I would pray that something like that could never happen again. Not here. Not in this country. But I didn't know if that was why Kathryn was asking.

I looked at her in the rocking chair next to me. We were both rocking, each holding a baby. Outside the snow was still falling. In the kitchen, someone was preparing food for us. She said, "I should sing to them more. Like you used to sing to us."

The songs I used to sing! All folk songs or rock and roll. "Summertime" was the only lullaby I knew but the lyrics had scared Kathryn. "Don't sing that part," she used to say, when it was time for *Nothing's gonna harm you*—because, of course, why promise something won't happen unless it could?

On the last morning of the residency, two women students had sung, impromptu, acapella, Sylvan Esso's song, "Come Down" as a parting gift for all of us. The lyrics were about a mother washing her child's hair in a river. The students had stood in the best acoustic spot of the studio facing one another, their eyes sometimes open, sometimes closed, the long pauses between phrases, their voices winding above and below one another's in harmony. It was like listening to water, in a way, or to your own memories. This would be a good song to sing to children. It felt holy, like communion, there in that studio of people, the forest just outside, the caldera full of water, blue in the summer but gray now beneath the winter sky.

And, of course, on that morning, I had longed to see Kathryn. It had been only four days since she'd given birth. I'd asked them to sing the song again, the words so simple, filled with longing, a longing for healing. I started to cry, although I didn't want to cry, but I did because of the pure beauty of their voices and the images evoked, the river through the trees, my hands washing my daughter's hair when she was little, her long hair now and how I longed to run my fingers through it. When the song ended, I opened my eyes. I was not the only one in tears.

CAUTIONARY TALES

When I return home from a writing conference in Iceland—I've been gone a little over a week—Kathryn's twin babies are lying on the living room floor. It is early June. They are just beginning their eighth month of life. When they see me, they start waving their arms and legs in greeting, but their bellies stay firmly on the floor. They look like they are paddling invisible surfboards on an invisible sea. If Baby A's desires could control his body, he would levitate into my arms. Baby B beams like a little Buddha.

I've been in a dark mood since the babies were born on the eve of Trump's election, the whole of their short lives so far overshadowed by worries about the repeal of health care and the dismantling of agencies designed to protect public education, the environment, and Civil Rights. I'm old enough that my fears are historically grounded. On my tenth birthday, in 1964, three Civil Rights workers were "disappeared" by the Ku Klux Klan in Mississippi for registering voters. A few years later, I remember the black girls in gym class talking about George Wallace; they joked that their bags were packed. I remember two other girls, both white, in high school going to Phoenix for abortions that I now realize must have been illegal. In the '70s and '80s, I waited for hours, sometimes days, in public health clinics for my children to see a doctor. I knew what it was like to have to decide between paying the electric bill or buying asthma medication for my son. I had seen pictures of the Cuyahoga River in Cleveland on fire. I had drunk water from polluted aquifers in Tucson, pollution that probably contributed to Fernando's death. I had seen, firsthand, the air in Los Angeles. Yes, the air. You could see it. It was thick and the color of dirt.

No surprise that I come to think of the summer as being apocalyptic. There's going to be a total eclipse of the sun in August which seems like it should portend something. The local TV news predicts a million visitors to our area, the high desert of central Oregon, because we're so close to the path of totality. Flyers distributed throughout town encourage us to get prescriptions filled early, see a doctor if we need to, store extra food, stock up on bottled water and toilet paper, buy batteries for our flashlights, fill our cars with gas. Kathryn's husband, Justin, a commercial fisherman who has been out on the choppy seas near Alaska ever since I returned from Iceland, tells us we should do all of this, especially since fire season has started early this year.

Of course, also in August, even before the eclipse, even before the smoke gets so bad, North Korea has started test-firing missiles and Trump is threatening to answer with "fire and fury the world has never seen." White supremacists in khakis and sports shirts are marching, unmasked, with tiki torches in Charlottesville, yelling Nazi slogans like "Jews will not replace us!" and "Blood and Soil!"

So here we are, Kathryn and me and the babies, sequestered in our 91%-white-bubble-of-an-affluent-town, which no longer seems, because of the news and the fires, so innocent and safe and pastoral. Here we are, sleepless with sleepless babies, watching, waiting for the smoke to clear.

Our only respite seems to be to give into the illusion that we can protect the babies, that all is normal as long as we keep them inside, and so that's what we do. Their whole world consists of the baby-proofed living room and nursery; their mother and the dog and I, the only other inhabitants. The trees and deer and quail outside the sliding glass door may as well be on the TV screen.

The TV is the bigger draw, of course. Both babies are mesmerized by Gwenyth Paltrow's voice as she recites "How Do I Love Thee?" And Baby A moves his arms wildly as if he's conducting whenever he hears Mozart. Even though he is smaller, he has round cheeks now that he's gained some weight, and dimples, a winning smile. He frog hops across the floor. His younger but bigger brother, Baby B, can crawl. When Baby Lamb comes on the TV, he stops what he is doing and gazes at the screen. Baby B is in love with Baby Lamb and with his father's voice on the phone. Baby A is in love with his mother. He puts his forehead against hers, his nose against hers, and when he tries to kiss her with his open mouth, it looks as if he is trying to devour her.

During the week before the eclipse, we wonder if we'll even be able to see it. The sky is so dark with smoke from the forest fires around us, so thick with smoke that the fire lookouts can't see a new plume for yet another fire. By the time they spot the new one, it's out of control. This is the fire closest to us. Kathryn watches the news for containment numbers. To the north and west of us campgrounds, resorts, and homes are being evacuated. Still, all around us, strangers are parking campers and SUVs bumper to bumper until they line the narrow streets. The people have come for what they might not be able to see. They fill parking lots and grocery stores and restaurants.

The sun, a shrunken plum, is visible only near sunset. It shimmers like a mirage of a sun between the tops of the pine trees. When I take the dog for his evening walk, my eyes sting. I hold my hand out. White ash falls like tiny, toxic snowflakes.

It's a hot, dry, thick smoke that settles between the trees and in our lungs. Visibility is less than a mile. Air quality, we are told, is worse than in Shanghai. Like smoking a pack of cigarettes a day. This is how they ought to measure air quality—instead of in colors, yellow, orange, red, like terrorist alerts—in terms of disease probability.

Lack of sleep, of course, is a major contributor to our anxiety. Like me, Kathryn is not a person who worries without reason. She is logical. She does her research. She weighs variables. After all, she is a nurse. And like her father, she trusts her intuition. But she has been sleep-deprived for essentially eight or nine months, longer if you consider how hard it must be to sleep when you have two babies vying for space inside your body. And it has only worsened since Justin left for Alaska. Maybe because they miss their father, who had been taking care of them during the day while Kathryn worked, the babies have been taking turns waking up in the night, wanting her to breastfeed them back to sleep.

"I feel like a giant pacifier," she tells me.

The babies, we learn, are going through a sleep regression, a time of rapid brain growth. They are learning so much when they're awake—how to sit, how to get back on their tummies from sitting, how to crawl, how to grasp with their hands, how to release whatever's in their hands, how to pull themselves to standing, how to say mamamama, how to make the sign for milk. I never realized it before, but being a baby is hard work. All of these things they're practicing while awake, their brains are rehearsing when they're asleep. Those neural pathways have to become so ingrained, after all, that they will eventually be able to do all of those things—sit, stand, walk, grasp, release, lie down—without conscious thought. But the problem is, because their REM sleep is so active and because they cycle through REM every twenty minutes—as opposed to once an hour for most adults—they are easily startled awake during these sleep regressions.

We read up on sleep training, which is a new thing: you can hire people to teach your baby to sleep. "Studies reveal that parents lose six months of sleep during the first twenty-four months of their infant's life," one site notes, a site that charges $495 a night for someone to come in and train your infant to sleep. How much for twins? We don't inquire. But judging from the plethora of sites, sleep training is a trend.

Most sleep trainers use the Ferber method, also known as the "cry-it-out" method, where you let the babies cry for longer and longer intervals until they "put themselves to sleep." No one knows whether they just exhaust themselves or actually learn to self-soothe. The method seems to "work"—except for with infants who get so upset that they throw up—but there have been no studies to show how or why or if there are long-term side effects or if other methods, which also seem to work just as well, are better because the parent is actually helping the child learn to self-soothe.

Perhaps you are paying someone $495 per night to ignore your baby.

This seems to me, as with so many things now, like choosing expedience over long-term results or, more importantly, regardless of long-term consequences.

And how do you do this with two babies? When B starts crying, A is immediately alarmed and joins in. On the other hand, when A starts crying, B observes for a while, as if to say, "Wonder what's up his butt?"—and then eventually joins in. There is no such thing as allowing a twin to cry it out. You will only end up with two screaming babies. The house is not large enough to separate them. When A cries, you can hear it in the front yard.

And crying is not necessarily a good thing in babies. My mother used to say that crying is how they exercise their lungs. Okay. Maybe true. But an extended bout of crying is physiologically stressful for babies. According to Dr. Sears, whose book we consult daily, excessive crying lowers their growth hormones, but increases their cortisol levels, blood pressure, and heart rate—the latter two evident in both A and B, in my opinion, as well as in my own blood pressure and heart rate.

The evolutionary mother in me kicks in when I hear that tone of distress. We are biologically wired to respond to babies' cries; their survival depended on it. The survival of the tribe depended on it. There is a reason people strapped their babies to their bodies, day and night: in case they had to leave the premises quickly.

Kathryn begins to worry about the uncleared brush around her house. If the fire gets closer, we could try to wet it and the roof with the hose, but what about low water pressure? Everyone will be trying to do the same thing. With the high temperatures and smoke, we worry about the AC going out—but then we could relocate to my downstairs apartment, which is always cool, even with the windows closed. We worry, if the fire gets too close, if we're told to evacuate, how will we be able to do that if the roads are clogged with a million visitors? They've said it could take eight hours to travel the thirty miles north to the airport. If we try to evacuate and her car runs out of gas, how far and how quickly will she and I be able to carry the babies in their packs—this is what I worry about, my own fallibility—and how will we protect their tender pink lungs?

I look it up. A wildfire, depending on the wind, can travel as fast as 6.7 miles per hour in a forest; in grasslands, 14 miles per hour. I know my walking speed, without a baby strapped to me, without hills, is about 4 miles per hour. Tops.

One day, when I come over to help with naptime, she says, "I keep wondering if I'd be able to suffocate them so they wouldn't have to feel the pain of burning."

I've wondered about this, too. I've wondered how close the fire would have to get. I've wondered why she had to inherit my imagination. I've wondered if there are mothers who don't worry about such things.

She tells me there is a crawl space in her closet that goes beneath the house. "Maybe that would be the safest place," she says.

I see she has given this serious thought. But the fire would have to be licking at the floor above us before I could give up hope of rescue for the babies. And her. She's my baby. I would have to smell my own hair burning. But I would have to do it before I passed out from smoke inhalation. And what about her dear dog, Ollie? Whom I love more than I love most people.

I look at the juniper trees outside the window. A third of their needles are brown and dry. The juniper, pine, aspens, they're the same natural vegetation that grows in higher elevations in Arizona, but this town is green, artificially so: no xeriscaping here, lawns everywhere, golf-courses, all watered because a river runs through it. This is the desert. I can see it because I'm from the Sonoran Desert. I can see the way they take water for granted, but I'm not sure the people living or moving here see that or understand what it means. The snow pack can disappear; rivers can go underground, disappear completely. This part of Oregon, like most of the West, has been in a drought for at least seven years. Scientists say a mega-drought is coming to the West; some say it's here. The current drought is occurring at the same time that there are dramatic changes in Western forests, which are conducive to these massive fires. People who have lived here their whole lives tell me this is the worst fire season they've ever seen.

We should leave, I think. I go online to see if there are vacancies on the coast for the eclipse. No, all booked up. Besides, there are fires in the mountains we would have to cross to get to the coast. Some of the passes are closed. What about a trip to Boise to visit her brother? No, there are fires between here and there, fire all around us. No escape. "Besides," Michael tells us, "Boise's air quality is red."

I decide to stay the night, both in case we have to evacuate and because it's the hardest time for her to be alone. I'll stay overnight and go home in the mornings, to my apartment, as if it were my office, to work. And then I'll come over late in the afternoons to help with dinner and to spend the night again.

Getting the babies to fall asleep is not the problem. The problem is getting them to stay asleep. According to "attached parenting" theory—and should there be any other kind of parenting?—if the baby wakes in the middle of the night, someone who is not the mother is supposed to try to rock the baby back to sleep. Rock. Walk. Wrestle. Sing. It's called "wearing the baby out" and some people literally wear the baby in a sling and walk around the house and do chores until it falls asleep. Whatever it takes. Just don't take the baby and give it to its mother if you're trying to wean it from night feeding.

But the twins are preemies. We don't want to deprive them of food, especially not the little one whose size doesn't even appear, yet, in any percentile on any growth chart in any doctor's office. We decide the first time they wake up, I'll try rocking them back to sleep. If that doesn't work, we'll assume they're hungry and I'll give them a bottle and then rock them to sleep. I will only take them into her if it's four in the morning or later so that she can nurse them back to sleep. Theoretically, in a week, they should be weaned from constant night-feeding and will wake, at most, once a night—unless you consider 4 a.m. night (which I do) and then it would be only twice a night. Each. So four times a night, total. (Math skills are crucial with twins.)

Even though it's been thirty-seven years since Kathryn was an infant, I can wake in the middle of the night, heat a bottle, change a diaper, feed the baby, burp the baby, and rock the baby back to sleep in forty-five minutes. This is all with operating by night-lights, only one eye open, so that I can go right back to sleep myself. Theoretically, if one baby wakes and then the other one doesn't wake until an hour later, in two hours, I can get both babies changed and fed and rocked back to sleep. Then Kathryn can get up early with them and I can sleep in. This works the first night. Kathryn gets seven hours of sleep in a row for the first time in months.

The day of the eclipse offers an almost miraculous reprieve from smoke and worry: blue skies. Not only that, but the babies fall asleep. One sleeps for hours, a marathon nap, unheard of in his short life so far. Kathryn and I actually get to sit outside in the backyard with the baby monitor, holding our eclipse glasses to our faces so we can watch the moon swallow the sun. The air gets noticeably cooler. The birds quiet, the shadows lengthen. The colors are underwater colors. We are in the 98.6 percent zone and so, we wonder, what difference could 1.4 percent make? Later, we learn it makes a big difference: seeing stars in the daytime instead of mere underwater colors and long shadows. But we don't care. We enjoyed our 98.6, our clean cool air, clear skies, and quiet babies.

Our system doesn't work every night. Who knows why? They are teething. They miss their father. They have gas. Their little brains are in overdrive. There are nights when our system works, and there are nights when they take turns waking up every hour or so, or when they both wake up at once, or when the little one is inconsolable unless he is allowed to nurse. He purses his lips, turns his head, arches his back, and screams if offered a bottle. He almost jettisons himself out of my arms. He wants his mother.

Babies cannot be spoiled. They cry because they need something and being held and comforted is a need. If you don't meet their needs, they eventually learn that they are powerless. After all, what is the point in trying to communicate if no one responds? This feeling of abandonment—what else can it be called?—is one of the possible psychological side effects noted by critics of the let-them-cry-it-out method, although no one knows how to test for it.

Ollie paces and then, sighing heavily, lies down in whatever room a baby is being comforted. I sometimes wonder if he can sense a potential failure of patience. But, oddly, I never feel frustrated or helpless as I did when Kathryn was little and had colic. Maybe it's because I'm the helper and not the mother. Maybe because there's something seductive about feeding and holding and rocking a baby at night: the darkness closes in, the world is hushed, the baby snuggles in, and whatever is wrong with your heart begins to heal. Maybe it's because when you're twenty-four and you can't "fix" the baby, you feel as if this will go on forever, but when you're sixty-three, you know it won't.

And you know you will be mostly helpless in the face of your child's suffering, no matter how old your child comes to be. You can be the comforter, the loving arms, the cooing voice, but you can't change anything, not even something as simple as a gas bubble stuck beneath the ribs. It's okay. I find myself saying this to the babies all the time: it's okay, it's okay, it's okay. A meaningless mantra. But they seem to understand that something is almost over.

And that's what we think about the smoke. That it will go away soon. But after the eclipse, it's even worse. We no longer worry about it, of course, because we know we can evacuate if we have to, but we still can't take the babies outside. The smoke hangs over everything. It's oppressive. Depressing. Feels ominous. Even at night, I feel as if I'm standing next to a campfire and the wind is blowing the still-hot smoke directly in my face. There is no moving away from the fire.

One afternoon, as we watch the news about the white supremacists in Charlottesville, Kathryn says, "Sometimes you have to fight hate with hate." To hear her say this makes my heart hurt. Probably because I know it's true: this is the world the babies have been born into.

One afternoon, as I help Baby B use the gate to pull himself to standing, I am thinking about all the work waiting for me on my desk at home. I wonder why I have replicated my old life, where I am, again, torn between taking care of others and teaching and writing.

One afternoon, Kathryn and I are sitting on the couch, too tired to do anything as constructive as clean house or do dishes. A nap is our main goal for the day. Suddenly she starts flailing her arms and legs in the air, "Help me! Help me! I'm a baby! I have poop in my pants!" I start doing the same thing. "Feed me! Feed me! I'm hungry!" "I have a tummy ache! Burp me!" Both of us flailing our arms and legs and laughing. "Rock me! Rock me! I'm tired!" If the babies realize we're making fun of them, they show no sign and just keep doing their baby-yoga-thing on the floor. But the dog is alarmed at this sign of hysteria. We have to stop when he starts barking. "It's okay, Ollie," I say. "It's okay, it's okay, it's okay."

It's early September now as I write this and, although we can go outside, we can still see and smell smoke. The prediction is that smoke from fires will affect our air quality well into October. Seattle, Boise, and Denver may have to wait for the first snowfalls in the mountains before their air will be clear of ash and smoke. This is not the worst fire season in recorded history, but close, and it is "climate enabled" if not caused. There are 80 large wildfires covering 1.4 million acres across the western United States. Oregon is one of the states hardest hit; Montana, the hardest, with 26 fires. There are also blazes across the rest of the US, Canada, South America, Russia, and Europe. Drought, dry fuel, high temperatures, low humidity, wind: perfect conditions for fires to spread rapidly. In Portugal, sixty people died while trying to evacuate. In Europe, a heat wave of above 100 degrees Fahrenheit has been named Lucifer. They didn't have to name it Lucifer. With babies, there are enough things to worry about without invoking Lucifer.

There are no trees left to burn in Iceland. Or very few. The story is that the Vikings cut them all down for building materials and for fuel. This started in the ninth century, when one quarter of the countryside was covered in trees. Within three centuries, the land was almost completely deforested. Their sheep ate all the nubs that might someday become trees and the soil eroded. There were more volcanic eruptions and more ash, which led to more erosion, and the strong winds, along with the loose soil, further damaged the land, making agriculture nearly impossible and leading to a very low standard of living. In 1882, according to an article I read by Henry Fountain, there was a huge sandstorm that lasted for two weeks. Sheep died because their wool was so weighed down with sand that they couldn't reach shelter. A lake was completely filled in with volcanic sand, the dead trout left lying on the top. Since then, the Icelanders have been trying to reforest, but trees grow very slowly there: in the last 100 years, since reforesting has become a priority, they've gained only one half of one percent.

The dramatic, austere landscape of Iceland is, therefore, a kind of man-made or maybe, more accurately, a man-unmade environment. It was covered with a sheen of green when I visited, so beautiful next to that black rock. Like others, I suppose, I wanted to see the glaciers, the waterfalls, and the black beach of Reynisdrangar, with its tall columns of basalt standing in the sea. I wanted to see the island before it melted into the water or was swallowed by it. But I didn't realize how fragile the ecosystem was. The glacier I visited, Mýrdalsjökull, is losing 100 meters a year, which means many things: in 200 years, it will no longer exist, but the melting ice—because ice weighs more than land—means that the land will rise and when the land rises, there will be increased volcanic activity. Iceland may not sink into the sea, after all; it may explode out of it. Now, when I think of the land of fire and ice, I think of it as a warning, a cautionary tale.

DIE DIE DIE

It was 1980, I'm going to guess. I had the news on while I was making dinner, so I must have been listening while I cooked and then peering into the living room to see specific coverage. We had a very small black-and-white TV then, one I could put into the closet when I got tired of its noise. I remember Michael was sitting rock-still in front of it. He turned to me and asked, with quite a bit of anguish for a five-year-old, "Why is it men who always do the bad things?"

This was long before any of us could ever have imagined someone going into a school with an assault weapon and shooting children. I mean, there was that one white guy in 1966 who'd climbed up the bell tower in Austin and opened fire on the students, killing fourteen and wounding more, and then in 1970 the National Guard had killed four student protestors at Kent State, and the Mississippi State Police had killed two at Jackson State. Still, those seemed isolated incidents, nothing like the regular fare since Columbine.

Now we say: Where? How many this time? How old?

Yesterday, as Kathryn and I were watching the footage of the high school shooting in Parkland, Florida, where seventeen people were murdered, I told her that story about her brother. I said, "Little boys are so sweet."

We were both thinking, of course, of her twin toddlers, not even eighteen months old, and how when you hold them, they gaze into your eyes and twirl your hair with their fingers, how they rub their faces against yours in affection. I was also thinking of Michael's sons, nine and twelve, and of Michael, himself. Five sweet boys.

As a friend of mine says: boys wear their hearts outside of their bodies.

~ ~

In November 2016, when Michael came with his family to visit for Thanksgiving, I kept hearing the older boy, as they were playing video games, saying to the younger one that he would sacrifice himself. Every time I heard him say

this, even though I knew it was his character he was talking about, I felt he was
being noble and sweet. They take their games very seriously, after all, and dis-
putes can erupt in fistfights. This Thanksgiving, as I sat down next to William
and watched him play, I realized his character—or avatar?—was really a suicide
bomber.

This game, I don't know how to explain it if you've never played one, is not
realistic. It's like you are in the world of the game—not watching from outside,
but inside the head of the avatar, a first-person protagonist. You see only what the
avatar sees so, generally, down the sights of the barrel of a weapon. As the avatar
rushes down a street, the landscape rushes by as if in your peripheral vision. In
this particular game, what the avatar sees is a bunch of blocks rushing by or,
more accurately, buildings suggested by line drawings. Your mind has to fill in
the details and this must draw you even more deeply into the imaginary because
you participate in creating it.

"Where are we?" I ask William.

"In a mall," he says.

"A shopping mall?"

"Yeah," he says, not missing a beat. We are hurrying, scurrying on, staying
close to what I guess are walls for cover.

"So, this is about urban warfare?" I ask.

"No," he says.

"But we're in a shopping mall," I say.

William is smart. Only twelve, he's been reading at the high school level for
a few years. He can read a thick novel a day, two if he doesn't have to go to school
or is on restriction from electronics. He has been saying to me, since he was two
years old, "Well, actually, Nana. . ." and thus, politely, correcting my errors in
many matters, even physics and the anatomy of birds.

"Okay," he says, "Yeah. I guess you could call it urban warfare."

"What are we doing?" I ask him.

"Well, we want to get in a crowd before we detonate. We want to take out at
least four or five others."

"We're a suicide bomber?"

"Well, it's just, technically, the more we take out, the more points we get."

"But we die, too, so we're a suicide bomber."

"Okay. Yeah." He shrugs. Then, "Watch out! See that guy up there? He's a
sniper. Snipers are the bane of our existence."

I did some research on suicide bombings for a book. They cause a lot of eye
injuries, I wanted to tell him, because when people hear the noise, they turn to
look in that direction. They open their mouths to scream and, sometimes, bone
fragments from the bomber get lodged in their lungs.

~ ~

When I was a child, I would not have known what a suicide bomber or even a sniper was. Now I cannot see a video game except for through the lens of reality and, therefore, the lens of suffering. I cannot divorce the game from the events that gave rise to it in the first place. But William can because, to him, I guess, it's just a game. A video game may not be art, but it is mimetic in its own way.

When Michael was little, I made him "stun guns" out of clothespins. I told him they would just put the enemy to sleep, so he could get away. This seemed to satisfy him. When he had little plastic cowboys and Indians, and his cowboys, the good guys, were dispatching the Indians, I tried to explain the history of the West. But how do you explain genocide to a four-year-old? Soon the Indians were retaliating and winning. When I asked my mother-in-law what she thought about giving him toy guns, she said, "He knows it's just make-believe." And so I let his fourteen-year-old uncle, who often babysat him, make them guns out of wood and sticks and they, along with Michael's aunt, who was eight, would chase one another around in elaborate games of hide-and-seek.

Now, when I watch Michael's sons, they argue about who gets the Nerf gun that holds the most "bullets," so essentially the dispute is about the magazine, the firepower. Why is it that their worst fights erupt over guns or video games? That Gavin's worst nightmares happen after he watches movies like *Star Wars*? They don't watch the news, so I'm not sure if they're even aware that our country has been involved in a war for longer than they've been alive, but they do know what suicide bombers are and snipers.

Am I overthinking it? But I wonder, sometimes, what kind of inchoate messages are coming down to them? Something about dominance. Something about violence as a form of power. Something about anger as a thing that makes you strong and even excuses aggressive behavior. Something about masculinity that, for Michael, took the form of the question: "Why is it men who always do the bad things?"

~ ~

Emma González's body was vibrating with anger in her first speech after the mass murder in Parkland, Florida. Her head shaved, her expressive face, her voice hoarse, she was wiping away tears as she spoke. When she addressed those who had criticized the students, saying they had ostracized the shooter, her voice became even more raw with anger. Still, she spoke: "You didn't know this kid. We did."

If you are a parent, chances are you know this kid. When Kathryn was a young teenager, probably fourteen, her boyfriend, who was older, was one of those kids. When she broke up with him, he came into our house, while she was alone, and slit his wrists in front of her. They weren't deep cuts, but she felt threatened, afraid he would turn the X-Acto knife on her. She remembers embracing him and telling him that she loved him while she slowly walked him to the door, thinking, the entire time, please don't cut me, and then she shoved him out of the house and locked the door between them.

When she still refused to see him, he got three of her girlfriends to break into the house with him, again when she was alone, and threaten her. She locked herself in our bedroom and wouldn't come out. There was no phone in our room; there were no cell phones. She listened as they continued to yell at her and call her names, as they banged on the door. She listened as they started to wreck our house, taking food from the refrigerator and throwing it all over the kitchen and living room. We decided never to leave her home alone again. I withdrew her from school and started taking her with me to the classes I was teaching at the university.

Around this time, the boy's mother called me and said she was worried. Her son had been acting out more than usual. He would not obey any of their rules. "My husband has guns," she said, "and they're locked up, but I'm still afraid my son will get a hold of them." He had fought with his father the night before, trying to get the key. He had pictures of Kathryn hanging all over his room.

For months, maybe, he stood outside our house watching for Kathryn to come home every night. Sometimes we saw him standing down the street; sometimes we couldn't see him, but the phone would ring as soon as she walked in the door. At this point, we sent her to live with her aunt while we filed restraining orders, all the time knowing that a restraining order does not stop an angry person from doing what he is determined to do. Finally, he tried to stab his father—or perhaps he cut himself in front of his parents? Or he cut his father when his father tried to get the knife out of his hands? This is when they had him committed to a local psych ward. From there, even though he shouldn't have been able to, he still called her. He sent her a letter with his driver's license. Don't forget me, he wrote.

We borrowed money from my aunt. We moved out of that house. Kathryn enrolled in another school. She couldn't see any of her old friends, of course, not even the loyal ones, because we were afraid he would follow them to our house or he would talk them into giving him the new address or phone number. He was handsome and charismatic, true, but also many of the girls she knew blamed her for his suicide attempts and his aggression in general. If she had been more understanding, they assumed, he never would have done those things.

"Time and time again we reported him," Emma González said of the shooter. "No one was surprised that he was the one."

And this was true in our daughter's case, too. Few of the adults who knew him were surprised at his behavior. Person after person told us that he was a narcissist, that he felt entitled, that he had problems with anger. Even the school, even as they refused to expel him because none of this had happened on school property, even they acknowledged that he had a history of acting out. In our culture, male anger is often loud and explosive and dangerous and, although now we send them to classes to learn to "manage" it, we still accept it as an excuse for violence.

Emma González was trembling with anger, righteous anger, as she countered other people's assumptions about who was responsible for the shooter's actions. She was wiping tears away. She was passionate, yet articulate, and totally in control. I admired her.

Anger is simply an emotion, after all, like love or fear. What matters is not that you feel it, but what you do when you feel it. But with most school shootings, like most mass shootings, there is something cold and calculated. It's more like hunting than a crime of passion.

~ ~

In 2002, at the University of Arizona, where I taught, a student shot and killed three of his professors and then committed suicide. This incident did seem rooted in deep anger: he was middle-aged, ex-military, flunking out of nursing school and, instead of taking accountability for himself, he blamed these women for failing him. There may, of course, have been other underlying factors; regardless, the murders were carefully planned and carried out.

For instance, this guy had a concealed carry permit, five handguns with him, and 500 rounds of ammunition. Some think he was planning on killing some of the students, too, but then changed his mind and told them to leave the room after he killed their professors. He spoke to each woman before he shot her, asking her a question about her area of expertise. He shot each of them three times, twice in the chest and then once in the head.

After this happened, I got an email from a former student: *I hope nobody ever does something like that to you.* I wanted to be touched by this, but the email left me feeling uneasy. I hadn't seen this student for at least two or three years and, when he was in my class, it was clear that he was disturbed. He would sometimes get up from his desk and sit on the floor in a corner and rock himself there.

When I talked to him about it, he said he was on Accutane—an acne medicine which, I knew, could cause serious psychological problems—and sitting with the girls in his group made him so uncomfortable that he had to leave. They were so beautiful, he said, and they kept looking at him, they were disgusted by his skin. He and I would sit on a bench in the courtyard outside of the building and talk for at least a half an hour after every class. As much as I was concerned about him, I was also trying to ascertain if he could be a threat, especially to those girls he found so beautiful and judgmental.

When this student came back to class after a week or two of absences, with his forearms both wrapped in white bandages, he told me he'd been in a motorcycle accident. I thought maybe it had been a suicide attempt, either with a knife or a razor or his motorcycle. I walked with him over to student health to see a counselor. I advised him to make his health a priority and drop the class and take it when he was feeling better. He dropped the class—in fact, he may have dropped all of his classes—and I didn't hear from him again until after the shooting. After that, quite a few times, he would come by my office, which was in an isolated building, I was usually the only one there, and he would walk by the window, not recognizing me. Once he poked his head in the door. Still, he didn't recognize me. He mumbled, "Oh. Sorry."

When I went to the main office and asked about him, the administrative assistant said, "Oh, yes, he comes in asking for you a few times every semester."

"Does he ask about other teachers?"

"Yes. Often."

"All female?"

"Yeah," she said, looking a little surprised.

"I wonder if we should report him to the dean's office."

She shrugged, "We could. I guess."

And just what, exactly, could we report?

I'm not sure why he made me so uneasy. He was a lost soul, obviously. He couldn't even make eye contact with me. He desperately needed connection, especially if he was stalking me—and other women—after so many years. And stalking is what it felt like. I didn't reach out to him. I don't feel guilty about it because, as illogical as it may seem, that one sentence—*I hope nobody ever does something like that to you*—felt like a threat. Like it had occurred to him that someone might.

- -

"We have to pay attention to the fact that this isn't just a mental health issue," Emma González said. "He wouldn't have hurt that many students with a knife!

"How about we stop blaming the victims for something that was the shooter's fault?" she went on to ask. "The fault of the people who let him buy the guns in the first place?"

There is no way a teacher in America can enter a classroom without wondering how she might help her students escape, how she might escape herself. In the classrooms where I most often taught, there was no escape because the building was underground. The long corridor, which had classrooms on either side, was arranged in a large U, with one entrance/exit at each end of the U. There was one door into each classroom, sometimes two. At the bottom of the U, there was an auditorium that could hold about 300 people. There were no windows in any of the rooms, of course. There were no closets. There was no way to lock or barricade any of the doors.

In another building, one whole wall of the classroom was a huge window the width of two or three sliding doors. If someone started shooting through the glass from the outside, we would all have to drop to the floor and try to crawl through the one door out into the hallway. In other older buildings, classrooms might have a wall of windows out of which students could jump, but we might be several floors up. This is exactly what happened during the mass shooting at Virginia Tech. Professor Liviu Librescu, a Holocaust survivor, died holding the doors to his classroom shut so that his students could escape by jumping from the second story windows.

I've begun to wonder if architects are going to have to take school shootings into consideration as they design new buildings. If the shooter is coming from the outside, I know, some newer buildings, like where I teach now, can be put on lock down. But what if the shooter is already in the classroom? The lockdown, then, is designed to limit the murders to that one area? So the students in that area become a kind of sacrifice to save the others? A kind of collateral damage? What if there is more than one shooter? If the shooter is a student or ex-student, like the one in Parkland, he's been through the drills; he's aware of all of the emergency preparations and how to circumvent or use them to his advantage.

According to the National Conference of State Legislatures website, all fifty states allow citizens to carry concealed weapons if they meet certain state requirements. Since 2013, thirty-three states have introduced legislation that would allow concealed weapons on college campuses. In 2014, five states introduced legislation to prohibit concealed carry weapons on campus; none of those bills, prohibiting weapons, passed.

After the shooting in Parkland, I was watching the first reports with my son-in-law as we took care of the babies. A few of the newscasters and medical experts commented on the kind of damage these weapons can do to the human body, something I'd never before heard in television coverage, although I'd read about it. "About time," I said.

Justin, who hunts and is aware of the damage that different weapons and calibers can inflict, flinched. "I don't know if they should go into that on television," he said. "Think about the families."

Whereas a typical bullet, from a 9 mm, say, goes cleanly through the body, "looking like a knife cut," according to a doctor who'd been in Iraq, a bullet from the AR-15 explodes and fragments inside the body, shreds the flesh, turns bone to powder, causes massive bleeding. There is very little chance that the victim will survive.

Also, it seems to me, the families are not the ones being protected from this knowledge. It's the rest of us whose sensibilities are being spared. The families are going to find out exactly how extensive the damage was.

A friend of mine, who is an EMT, told me that according to new guidelines for first responders, they are no longer supposed to wait for the area to be secured. The wounds from these assault rifles are so devastating that they are to go in and try to perform triage immediately. Soon, she told me, they will hang tourniquets—just as they do fire extinguishers now—in all public places where a mass shooting is likely. Shopping malls. Concert venues. Movie theaters. Churches. Donut shops. Schools.

And, in fact, while there have been "Active-Shooter Training" sessions for a few years at the school where I now teach, this morning I got an email encouraging me to attend "Stop the Bleed" training. It detailed where the Bleeding Control Kits would be kept and what they contain. These are state of the art kits, with Israeli compression dressing; all AED—Automated External Defibrillator—boxes will contain them. Like Israelis, we are training for terrorist attacks on our soil but, here, the terrorists are almost always white, homegrown boys and men.

This last December, I sent my son a text:
Me: What is the name of the video game the boys were playing at Thanksgiving?
Michael: You mean, Die die die, cocksucking motherfucker?
Me: Yeah, that's the one, but when I googled it, the FBI showed up at my door.
Michael: LOL. Roblox is the platform. The game is called *Phantom Forces*.
Me: Special Ops?
Michael: It's a FPS.
Me: Oh. Ok. Thanks.

Michael: (First-Person Shooter)
Me: Oh, ok. I like your name better. I'm standing in the dog park, laughing.

~ ~

"I can't believe Michael and Sara let the boys play that game," Kathryn had said at Thanksgiving.

"I know," I told her, "I think it's odd, too."

"Especially Sara," Kathryn said, "she doesn't even like football."

One of us, I can't remember which one, asked Sara about it, and she said that at first she'd been really against it, but she figured that they would be exposed to games like that through their friends, so better to play it at home, where Michael can monitor it. After all, he loves to play video games, too. Always has.

Roblox games, like *Minecraft*, are games where the players construct the world, which does involve some creative problem-solving skills and the negotiation of community rules. I had watched William and Gavin play *Minecraft* before and they spent most of their time building their houses and trying to zombie-proof them. Gavin, in particular, loved to show me, step by step, how he was constructing each room in his house: bedroom, living room, kitchen. It all looked like Lego blocks to me, but he was very particular. Michael and the boys used to play together, each on his own device, sitting around the dining room table, and once, when Gavin was maybe five or six, he started freaking out because the zombies were coming.

"Deep breath!" Michael said, "Look up. Where are you? You're in the dining room. With us. There are no zombies."

In *Phantom Forces*, the "players" or the figures that you chase down and shoot look like Lego characters, just as they do in *Minecraft*. There is nothing realistic about the renderings of the setting or the characters and yet, when you shoot someone, the color red pools out.

And then all the YouTube videos that tell you how to play the games: I've watched several with Gavin. His favorite guy, from the sound of his voice, is in his twenties and from Britain. His shows are about *Minecraft* and I think Gavin likes them even more than the game itself. The guy gives advice about zombies and axes, etc., and shows you how to make cool "plays" and advance to the next level. These videos are pretty harmless, although laced with a little dark humor and enough swear words that Sara, when she overhears, will tell him to turn it off.

I, however, searched YouTube for *Phantom Forces* and posed the question "Which guns are best?" Even though, again, the images were clearly not representational, there was a human voice—again, an adult male voice, this time with an American accent—saying things like, "MP5 is my favorite gun, for its high fire rate, pretty solid damage, accuracy rate is not bad." All the time I was hearing this voice-over, I was also watching the speaker's view of his screen. "So I'm just walking around casually, looking for a couple of kills. . . oh, what's this? A fucking guy! Had to shut him down real quick, curb-stomp his face into the ground. . ."

I have no way of resolving my cognitive dissonance over my grandchildren, who are now twelve and nine—or anyone's children, really—watching videos like this one, which seem worse than the game itself. Certainly this guy's voice, on the video, dehumanizes people. He does not seem angry. Rather, his persona is kind of jocular but cruel, bullying, and matter-of-fact about it. His fascination with the weapons, which are not imaginary but correspond to real counterparts, signifies to me a deep longing for dominance, for power and control, and so it also signifies its opposite? A lack? A need? A fear? Why else the obsession with things that can harm others?

~ ~

If reading fiction, as brain-imaging technology has shown, can help people become more compassionate and empathetic—and after all, in reading fiction, we are deciphering marks of ink on a page—could playing games like this desensitize us? The answer from research on First Person Shooter games, so far, is yes, but they don't know to what extent or if the desensitization to the images translates into behavior. In the studies I've read, most of the subjects were in their twenties and thirties, and I, of course, am worried about children, whose brains are still very plastic.

But why couldn't video games be designed to strengthen the neural pathways connected to compassion, like reading fiction does? The player's imagination has to fill in gaps, just as it does in reading. In addition, the games are interactive and the player's physical actions are repeated over and over again until they're almost unconscious. This makes me think that playing these games must shape neural pathways even more effectively than reading does.

Still, it's hard to imagine an American market—because everything depends on the market, after all—for a video game that emphasizes compassion rather than aggression, collaboration rather than competition. What would such a game look like? How would one "win" it? Like all art, video games reflect our values and perhaps reinforce them in an endless feedback loop. This is why it might be important to ask: What do these games reflect back to us? How are they mirrors of what we believe, fear, and desire?

When I went to visit Michael in January, to help with the boys while Sara was out of town for ten days, the boys were no longer playing *Phantom Forces*. I'm not sure why and I didn't ask. For one thing, I had set aside the idea of writing an essay about it and, for another, I trust Michael and Sara's parenting decisions. Still, I wondered if it was because of the violence or because it was one of those games where players interact with other players from all over the world and so, therefore, it could be a problem in terms of strangers having access to the children and their information. I figured it was probably a little bit of both—or, maybe, the boys had become bored with that game. One can only hope.

For whatever reason, they were now playing a game where whales drop out of the sky. Gavin played this game on cross-country dates with a little girl, a family friend who lives in Brooklyn. Her voice was on a kind of speaker-phone. One night I heard her say, "Poison me." Gavin, evidently, didn't want to poison her. "No," she said, "go ahead and poison me." A friend told me later that this was probably a collaborative move that meant they would be able to go to the next level.

Some other bits of random conversations I overheard:

"A lightning gun. It's not the best. It shoots balls of lightning."

"I just killed someone with a stop-sign axe. It was gross."

"That's the zombie-apocalypse!"

"Does the dinosaur eat other people?"

I was just glad, frankly, about things as fanciful as whales falling out of the sky and swordfish swimming through the ocean, spearing donuts to get points.

For the whole ten days of my visit, William was procrastinating on a multimedia project about Mexico. He eventually wrote a passionate essay in defense of open immigration and the Dreamers, so passionate partly because he'd been watching videos on YouTube of people fleeing cartel violence, trying to make their way here on the train called *La Bestia*. "Watch this one, Nana, it's so sad." We watched together.

Only a few months later, William participated with his mother in the March for Our Lives. At the event in Washington DC, Emma González would stand silent for six minutes and twenty seconds, the time it took for the shooter to kill seventeen people. Her generation, it has been pointed out, is the first to grow up with mass shootings in schools as part of the normal landscape and with active-shooter drills as part of the normal curriculum.

I told William at one point during my visit that I didn't think Aunt Kat was going to allow the babies to play video games even though they obviously loved electronics and were always stealing our phones.

"Oh, Nana," he said, shaking his head, "they will not be of their generation."

I've been thinking, ever since, about what that might mean. Emma González and the other student activists, and William and Gavin, and even the babies, are all of that generation. And so is the Parkland shooter. They all play video games, or will. They all feel anger and every other possible emotion. There are pictures of Emma González hugging others and laughing. When William and Gavin first see you, they still want big hugs, and their faces are open and beaming. And the babies, who are now toddlers, like all toddlers in all generations, run to you like tiny drunken sailors. They lift their hands in the air to be held. They snuggle against you for occasional warmth and comfort. They have just learned to kiss.

THIRTEEN WAYS OF LOOKING AT GRIEF

When I first moved to Oregon, I joined a Spanish conversation group because I was lonely. It's not like Fernando and I spoke Spanish to each other. We didn't, except for when the kids were little, and it was almost Christmas. And it's not like he spoke Spanish often at all, even though it was his first language. Spanish was simply a part of our landscape. Hearing it was like smelling orange blossoms. Either could trigger a wave of homesickness and, sometimes, homesickness is just what you need: it reminds you that you belong some place, if not where you are. The other morning, I heard some guys outside my window speaking Spanish, and hearing it, its presence, reminded me, again, of its absence. It's almost as if I don't know what I am missing until I am missing it.

I am often surprised by grief, just as I can be surprised by hunger. I don't listen to my own body, I guess. I am surprised by the passage of time, too, by the fact that I am getting older and he is not, by the fact that it's almost Christmas again. It was twenty-two degrees when I walked the dog this morning. Little wonder all I want to do is stay in bed and sleep. Little wonder I want to start drinking at 4 p.m. because, yes, the sun is already going down. Little wonder I can't write anything. By now, you'd think I would recognize this long sad slide towards the anniversary of his death. In this case, this coming January, it will be the fifth anniversary: it seems impossible that I haven't seen him in five years and equally impossible that he ever existed.

⌐ ⌐

They say this about both grief and depression: you don't want to remember the painful things and so you can't remember the good things. Your memories flatten, lose their particularity. If you can't look backwards, you can't move forwards. The way Brené Brown puts it: "We can't selectively numb our emotions."

The way a therapist I was seeing, put it: Thanatos is the movement towards a time before birth, a time of no stimulation. No stimulation is not good for us, but neither is too much stimulation, which makes sense with grief, I suppose, since grief is really a state of over-stimulation: intense feelings, intense memories, love, regret, anger, desire, despair, longing—all too much—so there is then the long- ing for Thanatos, a complete lack of stimulation, which manifests in numbness and in a desire for the chemicals which facilitate numbness, like alcohol, opiates, or Valium. Morpheus as conduit to Thanatos.

After Fernando died, I started taking his painkillers along with my wine in the evenings so I could sleep. One night I dreamed he had come back. Are you in pain, I asked him. It's okay, he said, I have all that Oxi. Hmmm, I said, better call the doctor and ask for a refill. When I told Kathryn about the dream, she went to the medicine cabinet. "Have you taken all of these?" she asked me. "You're only supposed to take these if you're in pain."

"I am in pain," I told her.

"Not that kind," she said, putting the bottle in her pocket for safekeeping.

My worst fear when he died—besides that he would die—was that, know- ing my own fear of pain, I would erase him.

⁓ ⁓

The other day I was holding one of Kathryn's babies and he touched my bottom lip. Suddenly, I had this visceral memory: Fernando used to touch my bottom lip, so tenderly, just before he kissed me.

⁓ ⁓

I once read an essay by a man whose sister had committed suicide and he said he couldn't remember her. In his grief, he had erased all of his memories of her and, in a way, this was one of the worst things about her death. It was as if she had never been alive. But after he went to therapy, he could suddenly remember her very clearly, even the way her laughter sounded, the way she smelled, the way she moved through a room.

That is why I went to therapy. I wanted the sound of his laughter, a look of fleeting humor, but therapy didn't work for me. I don't remember any more than I ever did. I still have only photographs and memories like photographs.

What are the other ways people remember? Letters? No, we always lived together. No occasion to write. Voice messages? I found a few where he is asking me what I'm making for dinner. Or: what are you wearing? He would often text that right before he left work. He thought he was so sly.

I could think of a playlist of his favorite songs, I suppose, and listen to them. "Layla" would be on the top, both the original electronic version which, he said, showed the passion and anguish of the young man, and the quieter acoustic version, which was full of the older man's nostalgia and regret. "I don't want to fade away. Give me one more day, please." I guess it was Eric Clapton who ended up with George Harrison's wife, but in my dreams, I am never the one who has left Fernando. He's left me and I can't understand why he doesn't want me anymore. In my dreams, his death always translates to abandonment, as if he had some volition in the matter.

I have stories that bring him alive for others, but for me, they're stories. You want to capture that moment so you can remember, but once it's captured, it's static. I think it was the Hopis who believed in not writing down your stories because, in order to get into the next life, your stories need to still be growing, which means changing, which means living. You need, they believe, and I want, living memories.

My therapist said that the self exists only in relationship to others. When a person we love dies, the self we were inside of them dies—so it is also the loss of that self that we mourn.

⌐ ⌐

It's easy for me to remember the early years of our marriage, when the kids were young, perhaps because I've told so many stories about them. Our house and yard were always full of children and I would sit at my little desk in the kitchen and type my papers while they streamed through the house from the front yard to the back where they were building a fort. Fernando usually got home between two and four in the afternoon, depending on how hot the weather, and he would come in and make himself a bowl of cereal and sit at the coffee table and watch cartoons. Adán, a little boy from up the street, who was only three, very small, would knock on the door and ask, "Is Dad home?" And then Fernando would pour a bowl of cereal for him and they would sit and watch cartoons together. It was true, if there was a Dad of the neighborhood, it was Fernando.

Fernando and his youngest brother, who lived with us, used to bring home tarantulas from the construction sites. This was when the kids were in grade school. Tarantulas are very fragile creatures, as are all creatures, I guess, when their habitats are disrupted and they are sent into exile. Tarantulas often come out of their burrows in the summer, especially after the rains. They are not poisonous, although their bite can be dirty with bacteria, and they can shoot little tiny hairs off of their abdomens to paralyze prey or enemies. Anyway, Fernando and Jr. would bring them home, one or two at a time, in empty five-gallon paint cans. They'd teach our kids and the neighborhood kids to pet them gently and to let the tarantulas crawl up their arms. They had to be very careful not to drop them, as a fall, even from a short height, could be fatal.

At night, the tarantulas, who are nocturnal, used to scratch at the insides of the plastic paint cans. The sound was eerie. One night, after Jr. and the kids were asleep, Joe the Tarantula—they were all named Joe, as I remember—was scratching at the can as we were trying to watch TV and Fernando said, "Come on." We took Joe One, in his paint-can home, out for a walk to the desert a few blocks away. Fernando reached his hand into the paint bucket and carefully lifted Joe One out and set him on the ground. "Aren't you going to sing?" he asked me. "Sing?" "Born free. . ." And so, I sang, "Born Free" as Joe One and, later, all the other Joes, each in his own time, crawled off into the nighttime desert under a starry sky where Fernando and I stood for a while as he searched for constellations to show me.

~ ~

Every January, to prepare myself for the anniversary of his death, I do a ceremony of remembering. Each year, the ceremony is different but this year, the fifth, seems especially difficult for some reason, and so I am reading in my journal about a trip we took to Spain. The only journals I've ever written are travel journals and I did that so, when I returned, I could give them to my mother to read who, by then, was too ill or old to go on her own adventures. Mining these, I wish I'd kept journals all the time: daily life, an adventure as precious as travel.

First, I read about Madrid and it's true, just reading this after so long, certain feelings come back to me. It also seems true, what they say, that memory is a feeling of what happened; in this case, the feeling that I belonged anywhere as long as Fernando and I were together. By the time we arrived at the Plaza Mayor, after dinner on our first evening, it was full of people, some eating in the sidewalk cafés. We sat at a table near some classical guitarists, who were playing beautifully, as I remember, and ordered glasses of wine. After a while, another group set up at the café next to ours. Their instruments were their voices and their hands, a box for percussion. One of them put a board down on the cobblestones. He was the flamenco dancer. The two musicians had rich voices and I could hear the influence of the Arabic, one-word undulating over many notes. They took turns doing the percussion. I thought the dancer looked like a bullfighter. Fernando told me, later, that the couple behind us had been debating his technique, whether or not he was authentic. "Eh," I said, "what do they know?" "Well," he said, "what do we?" "True," I said, "but do we care?" "No," he said. He could always make me laugh. It was a beautiful night.

The next morning, as soon as we woke up, Fernando said, "This room is haunted. Last night, someone blew on my neck, but when I rolled over, it was not you. You were facing the other way."

There was a presence in that room or a feeling of a presence, I agreed, but I said, "Do you think there are any rooms this old that aren't haunted?"

But thinking about it, I knew there was a difference between haunted—unrest, disturbance—and simply a presence. It was true, there was something unsettling in that room. Perhaps it was the spirit of someone who had been burned to death in the Plaza Mayor during the Inquisition. Or of someone who loved that person? I wasn't feeling well in Madrid and I didn't want him to leave me alone in that room. It was better to be together.

~ ~

I remember a story in which a girl and her mother are staying in a hotel in Paris and the mother is deathly ill and the daughter leaves to find a doctor. But when she comes back, the hotel looks completely different, the room, what she thinks might be the room, is a different color, different furnishings, the people who run the hotel are different people and they say they have never heard of such a hotel, have never seen her mother, have never seen her. The girl searches. Her mother is nowhere to be found. The girl begins to wonder if she ever had a mother. This was the feeling in the Hostal de Macarena in Madrid, not one of a presence, but of an absence, an absence so complete that the place might dissolve into another dimension, taking everyone inside with it.

~ ~

In the Museo Reina Sofia, Fernando and I rounded a corner and through an arch saw Picasso's *Guernica*. It was what we had come to Madrid to see and yet we were not prepared for its power. It took up one whole wall of the room; there was nothing on any of the other walls. The first thing we noticed, besides its size, was that it was mostly black and white with subtle shades of blue, aquatint, which made it feel almost photographic, like reportage. Here, the result of a two-hour "bombing practice:" the bodies, torn apart; the arms reaching; the faces, all grimaces, all pleading. A woman holding the limp body of a child. A dim light bulb in what might be the center of a half-sun or a downcast eye. An oil lamp in a disembodied hand. The bull, in the upper left-hand corner, impassive, impervious, looking away from the carnage, was a symbol of Fascism, according to Picasso, and the horse, at the center, crying, was a symbol of the people. It was amazing how a painting that was so spare, really, almost a line drawing, and cubist, could so effectively render terror and grief.

As Fernando and I looked at the drawings and paintings in the adjacent "Picasso" rooms, we noticed that many of them, the ones in the room to the left of the *Guernica*, were labeled the *preparatorios* and the ones in the room to the right were the *postscriptos*. It seemed to me that the *preparatorios* were just that, sketches, to help him figure out individual parts of the painting and the overall composition, just as you would expect. But the *postscriptos* were more detailed, drawings or paintings of individual sections of the larger piece, and sometimes in color. The interesting thing to me: had he gone in and added that much detail or color to those parts of the *Guernica*, the balance of the part to the whole would have been thrown off, the emotional impact would have been destroyed. Picasso knew one of the hardest things to learn as an artist: when to stop. But I felt that, even though he knew the *Guernica* was finished, he had to do the *postscriptos* because he was not finished, not with the material, not emotionally.

⌁ ⌁

The "*Pacto de Olvidado*," or the "Agreement to Forget," started in 1975, the year of Franco's death, and has continued to this day. Even though the Spanish Civil War took only three years, from 1936 to 1939, it left more than half a million people dead, sent another half a million into exile, and led to Franco's almost four-decades-long fascist dictatorship. Neither the war nor the dictatorship is taught in schools and, although streets were renamed and monuments removed, the people who were in power stayed in power. The mass graves remained mostly undisturbed. No one wanted to remember such pain, of course. It was as if, in 1975, history started anew; the forty years before it, disappeared.

I wonder, when there is such enormous collective loss, if forgetting is the only way people can create a future together and so, publicly, they agree to forget. However deeply they may mourn, they keep the pact. Or maybe it's repression, whether of the official or unofficial variety? After all, the same people were still in power. Eventually, the forgetting leads to a kind of cultural erasure. Whole memories, whole years erased. And, maybe, even later, there will be a kind of cultural eruption of memory and then rupture? After we were in Spain, I read that, in Catalonia, they had started to exhume some of the mass graves. By 2017, Catalonia called for its independence.

But erasure is how I sometimes feel about my last five years. It's even as if there is a taboo about speaking of the dead, as if it's indelicate to bring them up after a certain number of years, yet another reason why I am deliberate about trying to remember.

In my first ceremony of remembering, I'd written an essay about the final days of Fernando's life and so for my second ceremony of remembering, in January 2015, I decided to send a copy of the essay along with a note to everyone who had loved Fernando and helped me through that first year. Somehow writing those thank-you notes took me through the difficult slide of sadness and helped me focus my attention not so much on my own grief as on gratitude for all the love that had somehow sustained me. In a way, it wasn't even actions or words that had sustained me but, instead, the continued existence of people who had loved him and still missed and remembered him.

I wonder now, thinking of the bombing of Guernica and of other times of mass murder, Wounded Knee, for example, where whole villages or towns have been wiped out, if that isn't what's most devastating: the lack of continued existence. No one left who loved the others. No one left to remember. During the Holocaust, for instance, I've read that, often, the person who was the most Aryan-looking in a community became the designated survivor and was told to do anything he had to do, including loading his own children into the trains bound for Auschwitz, in order to survive: to still exist so someone still loved them, so he could tell the story of what had happened and how they had been loved and how they had been lost.

᷍ ᷍

I thought we loved Spain. Later, years later, at a party, I would find out that Fernando liked Italy better. He was talking about Spain with a woman from Tucson, also Mexican American, who'd just returned, and she mentioned how badly she'd been treated. "Really?" I asked. "Why?" It was because the Spaniards really looked down on her, she said, they kept commenting on her Spanish. I remembered, then, that when we were in Zaragosa, Fernando had apologized to the taxi driver for his Spanish and the driver had waved his hand through the air as if he were swatting away a fly. "Oh," he said, "it's all the Spanish of Cervantes!"

When I told her that, she said, "Well, of course. They all say that. But the looks they give you!"

I looked at Fernando. Was he just being polite? We had laughed when the taxi driver said that and we'd had a lively conversation with him and he had given us a little impromptu tour of Zaragosa's sites as he took us to the train station. But here Fernando was, almost ten years later, agreeing with Terri about something I never knew he felt. An *extranjero* in the land of his forefathers. But, when I think about it now, why would you necessarily have an affinity for the country of your ancestors? Besides, he had ancestors from Italy, too. Plus, as he said later, when I asked him about it in the car, he'd never had a bad meal in Italy. Paella, eh, it was okay, but he was not so crazy about it.

These are the kinds of memories I wish could have more often, even though that last one makes me feel a little left out, the ones that come upon you when you haven't been thinking deliberately. Instead of the stories you've told many times, instead of the journal entries you can reread. Quick, living memories, like when the baby touches your bottom lip. Like the other morning, when the Allman Brothers' "Sweet Melissa" came on the radio. He loved that song and, suddenly, I remembered what it feels like to be standing next to him in a room full of sunlight right after he's come home from work, still smelling of dust and paint. Or, a few months ago, when I was asleep, I felt a presence in the room behind me. At first it scared me, but then I thought, Oh, it's Fernando. And, quickly, on the pillow behind my head, a light drumming with his fingers, tap a tap tap, like he used to do when he stood up from the kitchen island and then went into the other room. I had forgotten that he used to do that. Every time. An announcement: I'm off to the next thing!

Those are the memories that are missing for me, the most recent ones, those last five years before he died and the last five, now that he's been gone. The years that disappeared. *Los años desparacidos.* Like my therapist said, death had been at bay for all those years, yet we always knew it was coming. Fernando, I realize now, five years after his death, was my home. When I was with him, I felt most at home, most myself. And yet he is no longer. His death is my exile.

Once Fernando was standing in front of the stove. It was when we knew how sick he was, but he was still well enough to make his eggs exactly the way he liked them. He was wearing his red-checkered pajama pants and a dark green tee shirt Kathryn and I bought him in Prague. I loved that color on him. He made Kathryn promise that when I got a boyfriend, she wouldn't give him a hard time.

"Who says I'm going to get a boyfriend," I asked.

"She doesn't do well on her own," he said to Kathryn, not even looking up from the stove.

"How do we know I don't do well on my own? I've never been on my own," I snapped.

Why couldn't I have simply said, I don't want anyone but you?

One night, last October he visited me in a dream. We were sitting in water so blue it looked like a swimming pool, but I could hear rushing water behind us, like rapids or a waterfall. Clearly, we were sitting in a pool in the wilderness and, for a moment, I thought we might be swept away. But, no, the water was calm. I was not afraid. The pool was enormous, really, all we could see, like looking at the wide ocean. But there was an edge where the water fell off on the horizon and, all along that edge, sweeping the whole horizon, a thin line of intense light. Sitting next to me, although he was invisible and had no body, Fernando pointed to the line of light and said, That is what eternity is like.

ACKNOWLEDGMENTS

I would like to thank Autumn House Press for seeing the potential in this collection and, especially, Christine Stroud for her careful reading of individual essays and for her astute suggestions for revision. I also am indebted to her for helping me see the ways that the collection could be strengthened as a more cohesive whole.

The events in this book span forty years of my life and the essays evolved over a period of almost twenty years, so I am grateful to many people.

I am grateful to Barbara Cully, Susan Roberts, and Karen Brennan for their friendship and support through the years and for reading these essays in their many incarnations. Better friends I could not ask for: you helped me through illness and grief and doubt, giving me faith that these essays had a place in the world.

I want to thank Aisha Sabatini Sloan and Arianne Zwartjes for reminding me that "rigorous" and "artful" are not antonyms and for reading various versions of these essays and always providing thoughtful feedback. Debbie Weingarten, Hannah Ensor, Beck Iosca, Brian Blanchfield, and Molly McCasson all, I thank you all for giving me an ideal audience I could count on. Boyer Rickel, thank you for "ranking" the essays in order of "brilliance," a list I returned to whenever my confidence flagged. Polly Koch, wherever you are, thank you for telling me all the places that made you laugh.

Irene Cooper, Brigitte Lewis, Ally Bebbling, Tiffany McFee, and Lori Hellis thank you for the food for mind and body and soul and for giving me a writerly home in Oregon. Irene and Brigitte, thank you, also, for helping me polish and promote the book.

There are many others who supported my writing in many ways and whom I would like to acknowledge: Melanie Bishop, Ander Monson, Lisa Bowden, TC Tolbert, Ru Freeman, Ann Cummins, Nicole Walker, Jesse Sensibar, Pam Uschuk, Cynthia Hogue, William Pitt Root, Kristen Nelson, Carol Coryell, Kimi Eisele, Lisa O'Neill, Cara Blue Adams, Sheila Bender, Donna Steiner, Michael Cooper, Ellen Santasiero, Sally Hollister, Jennifer Delahunty, Kati Standefer,

Meg Files, Cheryl Diane Kidder, Michele Finn Johnson, Christine Krikliwy, Joseph Manning, Joe Parsons, and Justin Hargett.

I would also like to thank the journals—and their editors—in which many of these essays first appeared: *The Sun, Guernica: A Magazine of Politics and Art, Cimarron Review, The Louisville Review, River Teeth, Nimrod, North American Review,* and *Necessary Fiction.* Also, I'd like to thank *Cutthroat: A Journal of the Arts, Spork,* and *The Manifest-Station* for publishing earlier versions of a few of them, under different titles. I would like to acknowledge University of Iowa Press: parts of my memoir, *Anthropologies,* contain the seeds from which a few of these essays grew, especially the early ones. And my thanks to Heyday Press for anthologizing "The Motherhood Poems" in *New California Writing 2011* and to Lisa Bowden of Kore Press for republishing that essay in its blog, *Notes on the Mother Field.*

Finally, although I'm sure it's evident in the essays themselves, thank you to Fernando and to our children and grandchildren and to our extended family and to our dear dog, Ollie, who accompanied me on many walks while I puzzled over revisions.

NOTES FOR "WATER IN THE DESERT"

There were many sources for this essay. Some of them, like details about my brother-in-law's diagnosis of hemochromatosis and Fernando's liver cancer, come from lived experience. There are also many online sources about TCE contamination since it is one of the most commonly found chemicals at Superfund sites. Some of the data I found conflicts with other data; it's important to note the source and the date.

I feel it's also important to point out—since 95% of our drinking water in the US comes from ground water—that although they've been doing the "clean-up" of TCE in Tucson for over thirty years, recent articles point out that there is no "end in sight" because the pollution there is so extensive and the geology of the region makes cleanup even more complicated. Not only that, but they are now finding more cancer-causing chemicals, like 1-4 dioxane, in those wells. The process that works to eliminate TCE does not eliminate 1-4 dioxane, further complicating the cleanup and adding to its cost.

Although I consulted many sources, probably at least thirty or forty in order to fully understand the issue, I list below the sources that I found most valuable in writing about TCE contamination in Tucson.

First of all, all of Tucson owes a debt to Jane Kay, the reporter who investigated the causes of the problems with the water early on. Her series of stories on TCE were published in the *Arizona Daily Star*, beginning in May 1985. Her investigation provided documentation for what south side residents knew from experience: people were getting sick and dying from the water.

Another important source was the essay "Environmental Racism in Southern Arizona" by Jeanne Nienaber Clarke and Andrea K. Gerlak, which was collected in David E. Camacho's book *Environmental Injustices, Political Struggles: Race, Class, and the Environment*, Duke University Press, 1998.

Clarke and Gerlak's essay points out that while environmental racism may not have been a factor in the pollution itself, the official response to the TCE pollution was certainly rooted in racist attitudes: "It is critical to note that charges of racism developed primarily because Pima County's health director, an Anglo female physician, relied on the available epidemiological data to conclude that there were no connections between the incidence of serious illnesses among south side residents and their exposure to TCE." Instead, she assumed that their "lifestyle," was at fault; she told the "largely Latino audience [at a community meeting] that their diet was bad, they smoked and drank excessively, and didn't exercise enough." She never investigated the causes. Ed Moore, a controversial figure, who was on the County Board of Supervisors and represented this area of town at the time, agreed with her publically. Moore is famous in Tucson folklore for having said that south side residents got sick because they drank too much beer and ate too many "chilies and beans."

Many in the community, including one of the Latino members of the County Board of Supervisors, Dan Eckstrom, felt that racist attitudes were evident not only in the failure to investigate causes but also in the lack of action. He pointed out that "once the problem did become known, not enough was done. . . City officials wouldn't dare do the same thing in more affluent, white neighborhoods." Of course, Hughes Aircraft was one of the largest employers in Tucson and, as Robert F. Kennedy points out in the interview on *Grist*, in the conflict between poor communities and corporations, the communities are bound to lose.

As far as technical information about TCE pollution—for instance that "The permissible level of TCE contamination is less than the equivalent of 2.5 teaspoons poured into an Olympic-sized pool" and "On Evelina Street alone. . . thirty-four cancer cases were documented"—I relied on a series of slides in a class my daughter had taken at the University of Arizona, where she was getting her Masters in Nursing. The presentation was given by Christine Krikliwy, who had done her Masters in Public Health on the issue. Krikliwy not only gathered information about the contamination itself and resulting health issues, but she also collected oral histories of many residents. The slide presentation can be found online at http://coep.pharmacy.arizona.edu/tce/whatistce.html

Although the records of the court case with the original 1,600 complainants were sealed, the records of the appeals to those decisions were evidently not, as I found a pdf of the decision on line: APPEAL FROM THE SUPERIOR COURT OF PIMA COUNTY, Cause No. 251422. This document provided some of the most disturbing support, one, that prolonged exposure was not necessary in order for TCE to act as a metabolic trigger: "an individual's first exposure to TCE causes 'cellular damage,'" and, two, about long-term and even epigenetic consequences: "such cancers typically do not appear until ten to twenty years after exposure and may not be limited to one generation." Krikliwy's research and the article on *AlterNet* also support these conclusions.

In October 2015, I spoke by phone with Yolanda Herrera, who has been involved with the Unified Community Advisory Board (UCAB), a local organization that has fought for citizen's rights on issues of TCE for more than twenty years. I've quoted her in the essay and I subsequently attended a UCAB meeting where there were several representatives from federal agencies. Their attitude seemed to be that they had done what could be done and that no more should be asked of them and they brought graphs and charts to support their assertions. I was sitting next to Christine Krikliwy and, all during the meeting, she would scribble notes to me—for instance, that 1-4 dioxane is even more toxic than TCE—that threw their assertions into question. The representative from the Air Force, a white man in a very nice suit, did not, in my opinion, treat community members with respect. He dismissed their concerns. For instance, when an elderly man with a heavy Mexican accent asked a question about continued waste disposal at the Air National Guard, the representative told him, "There are four hundred pages of data at the Valencia Library. You can go and look it up."

I also learned, from attending UCAB meetings, that owners of private wells are not required to clean up or close their wells, which I guess we could see as their prerogative rather than as a public health issue except that some of these wells supply water to trailer parks. The owners of the wells also own the trailer parks and they are not required to disclose to their tenants that their water is contaminated. Of course, the tenants are low income. UCAB was trying to change these ordinances or at least obtain information that would allow them to make those disclosures.

Manuel Herrera, the community activist who is quoted in the essay, "Environmental Racism in Southern Arizona," may very well be Yolanda's father. I know her family, like his, like many others, has been devastated by illnesses attributed to TCE.

Other sources include:

"Agent Orange's Long Legacy, for Vietnam and Veterans" by Clyde Haberman, *The New York Times*, May 11, 2014.
"An Interview with Robert F. Kennedy, Jr., environmental advocate and Bush basher," by Amanda Little, *Grist*, July 14, 2004.
"Military Waste In Our Drinking Water," by Astra Taylor and Sanaura Taylor, *AlterNet*, August 3, 2006.
"Lengthy TCE Cleanup Sees Results," by Tony Davis, *Arizona Daily Star*, July 10, 2011.

NOTES FOR "LOS PERDIDOS"

I consulted at least thirty sources to write this essay, although much of that material was cut. In an earlier version, quite a bit of space was devoted to the damage caused by the cartels and by our complicity in the damage. Although very little of that version remains but because this issue is so important to me, I am going to provide a list of sources for further reading.

Anonymous: "Los Malos," translated by David Noriega. *Harper's Magazine*, Sept. 2010.

Gloria Anzaldúa, *Borderlands / La Frontera: The New Mestiza*. Aunt Lute Books, 1987.

Sarah Cortez and Sergio Troncoso, eds.: *Our Lost Border: Essays on Life Amid the Narco-Violence*. Arte Publico Press, 2013.

Kathryn Ferguson: *The Haunting of the Mexican Border: A Woman's Journey*. University of New Mexico Press, 2015.

John Gibler: *To Die in Mexico: Dispatches from Inside the Drug War*. City Lights Open Media, 2011.

John Gibler: *I Couldn't Even Imagine That They Would Kill Us: An Oral History of the Attacks Against the Students of Ayotzinapa*. City Lights Open Media, 2017.

Valeria Luiselli: *Tell Me How It Ends: An Essay in Forty Questions*. Coffee House Press, 2017.

Octavio Paz: *The Labyrinth of Solitude: Life and Thought in Mexico*. Grove Press, 1961.

AUTHOR BIO

Beth Alvarado is the author of three books: *Anxious Attachments,* a collection of essays; *Anthropologies: A Family Memoir* (University of Iowa Press); and *Not a Matter of Love and other stories* (Winner of the Many Voices Project Prize, New Rivers Press). Beth lived with her late husband and her two children in the Sonoran Borderlands for much of her life. She now lives in Bend, Oregon, where she teaches prose at the OSU-Cascades Low Residency MFA Program. She has an MFA from the University of Arizona and an MA in Literature from Stanford University. Her essays and stories have been published in many fine journals including *Guernica, The Sun, River Teeth, The Southern Review, Cimarron Review, Third Coast,* and *Ploughshares.* Her essays have twice been chosen as Notable by *Best American Essays.* Beth is on the editorial board of a new contemporary Chicanx anthology sponsored by *Cutthroat: A Journal of the Arts* and the Black Earth Institute.

NEW AND FORTHCOMING RELEASES

Blue Mistaken for Sky by Andrea Hollander

Thank Your Lucky Stars by Sherrie Flick

Luxury, Blue Lace by S. Brook Corfman ♦ Winner of the 2018 Rising Writer
Prize, selected by Richard Siken

Anxious Attachments by Beth Alvarado

The Last Visit by Chad Abushanab ♦ Winner of the 2018 Donald Justice Poetry
Prize, selected by Jericho Brown

Cage of Lit Glass by Charles Kell ♦ Winner of the 2018 Autumn House Poetry
Prize, selected by Kimiko Hahn

Not Dead Yet and Other Stories by Hadley Moore ♦ Winner of the 2018
Autumn House Fiction Prize, selected by Dana Johnson

Limited by Body Habitus: An American Fat Story by Jennifer Renee Blevins ♦
Winner of the 2018 Autumn House Nonfiction Prize, selected
by Daisy Hernández

Belief Is Its Own Kind of Truth, Maybe by Lori Jakiela

For our full catalog please visit: http://www.autumnhouse.org